THE ASPIRANT

Driven By Dreams

Becoming a Climber, Mountain Peaks & the Matterhorn

Roger E. Beaudoin, Jr.

Publisher's Information

EBookBakery Books

Author contact: 928reb@gmail.com

ISBN 978-1-938517-49-5

Black and White Interior Version
Author: 928reb@gmail.com

© 2016 by Roger E. Beaudoin, Jr.

ALL RIGHTS RESERVED

No part of this work covered by the copyright herein may be reproduced, transmitted, stored, or used in any form or by any means graphic, electronic, or mechanical, including but not limited to photocopying, scanning, digitizing, taping, Web distribution, information networks, or information storage and retrieval systems, except as permitted by Section 107 or 108 of the 1976 United States Copyright Act, without the prior written permission of the author.

View from Summit of Rimpfischhorn, August 1996. Photo Credit Roger Beaudoin.

Don Coddington on Matterhorn summit, photo on page 119 courtesy of Jean Pavillard.

Acknowledgments

I wish to thank: Klaus Scherrig for introducing me to the Alpine world and an excellent first adventure on Pollux; Richard Andenmatten, legendary guide with over 700 Matterhorn ascents, who's friendship and encouragement gave me the confidence to achieve my summit and many more; Viktor Imboden for pushing my comfort level and making me believe I could climb the Matterhorn's infamous Zmutt Ridge; Kurt Lauber for being resolute, defiant, a hero and inspiration; and Helmut Lerjen, for pushing my limits ever farther in 2000 and for an amazing Matterhorn ascent immediately after rescuing climbers in peril. I am eternally grateful for your guidance and friendship in the mountains.

Elizabeth Atwater for her interest in my story and ability to turn my writing into a compelling manuscript; Dr. Dirk Asherman for your expertise as an orthopaedic surgeon and your friendship... I never thought that I would walk normally again, let alone return to climb peaks.

Chris Profit for displaying my summit photo and Matterhorn SKI BAR menu in the North Wall Bar; Michael Grossman for your enthusiastic belief in this project, unfailing interest and expertise to guide the book to fruition; Conrad Jager for leading us safely on numerous exciting climbs and adventures in the White Mountains of New Hampshire; Chris Hayward and Bob Baribeau, leaders of Mahoosuc Mountain Search and Rescue for your incredible skills and judgment in the mountains, selfless devotion to helping those in need or peril and inviting me to join your ranks; Jim Noyes – you trained hard, seemingly had no fear and reached the Solvayhutte on your first attempt. You had the "right stuff" to summit with proper acclimatization; Ben Hamilton for your restless spirit, sometimes reckless enthusiasm and idea to return to the Matterhorn; Don Coddington for your persistence in chasing your own Matterhorn dream... 3rd times the charm! And to all those friends who lent encouragement, advice or contacts. You are too numerous to mention.

Dedication

To my wife Thea for allowing me to be me in pursuit of these adventures, for your belief in this project, constructive advice and encouragement to move forward and "Go Pro"!

To my children Samantha and Madison, may you be inspired to always follow your dreams wherever they may lead.

To my parents who taught me that anything is possible if I chase my dreams, and finally, for my sister Sandie, who never had the chance to follow her dreams. I love you all.

TABLE OF CONTENTS

Foreword vii
Prologue viii
Chapter 1 - Meeting the Matterhorn 1
Chapter 2 - Laying a Foundation 4
Chapter 3 - The Alpine Experience 11
Chapter 4 - Onward and Upward 23
Chapter 5 - The Only Peak that Mattered 41
Chapter 6 - I Find My Limits 57
Chapter 7 - Climbing Close to Home 69
Chapter 8 - A Sixty Foot Fall 93
Chapter 9 - Once More to the Top 101
Epilogue 123
Resources 127
Hikes & Climbs 129
Skills, Tips & Supplies 136
Training 141
Dictionary 144
Guides 146
About the Author 149

FOREWORD

"And so, the traditional inaccessibility of the Matterhorn was vanquished, and was replaced by legends of a more real character. Others will essay to scale its proud cliffs, but to none will it be the mountain that it was to its early explorers. Others may tread its summit snows, but none will ever know the feeling of those who first gazed upon its marvelous panorama, and none I trust, will ever be compelled to tell of joy turned into grief, and of laughter into mourning. It proved to be a stubborn foe; it resisted long and gave many a hard blow; it was defeated at last with an ease that none could have anticipated, but like a relentless enemy conquered but not crushed, it took terrible vengeance. The time may come when the Matterhorn shall have passed away, and nothing save a heap of shapeless fragments will mark the spot where the great mountain stood, for atom by atom, inch by inch, and yard by yard, it yields to forces which nothing can withstand. That time is far distant, and ages hence generations unborn will gaze upon its awful precipices and wonder at its unique form. However exalted may be their ideas and however exaggerated their expectations, none will come to return disappointed."

Edward Whymper, who on July 14, 1865, became the first climber to conquer the Matterhorn

Reprinted from *Scrambles Amongst the Alps in the Years 1860-1869* by Edward Whymper, ©2010 Nabu Press

PROLOGUE

Adventure is about challenge, danger, and adrenaline; a quest for the unknown. Inspiration allows the human spirit to revel in the possibility of extraordinary achievement.

For me, it was all about a mountain. It's not the highest, nor the most difficult or dangerous, although many climbers have died attempting to reach its summit. My inspiration, the Matterhorn, has a spirit which captured my imagination from the moment I saw it. Some consider it one of the seven wonders of the natural world. Its beauty and majesty transcend this world. I invested ten years before reaching the Matterhorn's summit. I persisted for ten years, despite frustrations over weather and the need to build my skills as a climber. Along the way I confronted my fear of the unknown, self-doubts and the Matterhorn's ability to intimidate. For the mountain is rife with stories about the legendary exploits of those who climbed her successfully; others tell of untimely deaths. Far better mountaineers than I scaled its awesome heights and never returned.

The dictionary definition of the word *aspirant* describes all of us who embark on climbs:

1 aspirant \ 'as-p(e-)rent *n*: one who aspires
2 aspirant *adj*: seeking to attain a desired position or status

In the world of Alpine mountaineering, the term refers to a prospective guide training to become an elite Swiss mountain guide. Aspirants study and must demonstrate proficiency in climbing techniques on snow, ice and rock. They must know how to evaluate weather conditions, avalanche and snow, be skilled in rescue techniques and in first aid. Once a guide's training program is complete, aspirants serve as apprentice guides for two seasons before being granted full guide's credentials.

For those of us who hike for fitness or adventure, climbing can teach us so much more about ourselves. An adventurer need not summit Everest or K2 to call himself a climber. From Colorado "14ers" to Wyoming's Tetons and many lesser summits, there are endless challenges in the mountains.

Climbing is familiar - primal. Scrambling over rocks and climbing trees are the simple adventures of childhood, and as a boy, I would escape for hours in a tree house or up on a high branch. As I got older, hiking and backpacking naturally led to climbing. I'd always been an avid hiker, but the Matterhorn inspired my quest to become a climber and to start my journey of self-discovery. What began as a young man's inspiration has persisted, becoming an enduring obsession.

I hope this book inspires others with an adventurous spirit to see that with training, good weather and a good guide, exciting summits can be reached safely. In fact, I hope this book inspires the reader to relentlessly pursue your dreams no matter what your "Matterhorn." Don't we all have goals we pursue? In some ways, I consider myself an aspirant; fueled by passion, driven by dreams and aspiring to reach the peak of the Matterhorn. It is in this spirit that I share my story.

> "By prevailing over all obstacles and distractions, one may unfailingly arrive at his chosen goal or destination."
>
> Christopher Columbus

> "Wanting something is not enough. You must hunger for it. Your motivation must be absolutely compelling in order to overcome the obstacles that will invariably come your way."
>
> Les Brown

> "To thine own self be true,"
>
> Polonius in William Shakespeare's *Hamlet*, frequently quoted by Wanda A. Beaudoin, the author's mother

1

MEETING THE MATTERHORN

Switzerland shaped my life. Its gorgeous scenery, spectacular mountains, and culture of efficiency has stayed with me, and I have returned many times to embark upon new mountain adventures. I eventually established a successful restaurant and bar at the base of a New England ski resort with a notably Swiss theme and ambiance, named for the Matterhorn. Although I have since sold the Matterhorn Ski Bar at Sunday River, it is filled with climbing memorabilia and photographs from my Swiss adventures.

The Matterhorn Ski Bar Sunday River, Maine

My first encounter with the Matterhorn came in the late 1980s. I was studying for a Master's Degree in Business at Babson College in Wellesley, MA. Babson offered students an opportunity to work as a summer consulting intern at a number of sponsoring companies and organizations throughout Europe and South America. I was thrilled when a global pharmaceutical manufacturer based in Milan, Italy selected me to research and create a United States subsidiary and to tie it structurally and legally to their other global subsidiaries. This was a monumental project that gave immense satisfaction. The Italian executives valued my opinions and treated me as an equal.

My first visit to their corporate base, Milan, introduced me to that cosmopolitan city, nestled in northern Italy with a distant view of the snow-capped Alps. I immediately embraced the culture, cuisine and language. It was both my fantasy and reality to wander the streets, coming upon new adventures in every neighborhood. I stayed in local university accommodations for eight weeks and even befriended native Italian students. As a Formula 1 racing enthusiast, I loved being in such an exotic car mecca, seeing more Ferraris, Maseratis and Lamborghinis than I was used to seeing at home.

The project was critical to my success at Babson and to the Italian company's success, so work was my priority and adventure was relegated to my weekends. For direction, I relied on a copy of *Let's Go Europe*, my bible for fun side trips. I had read about summer skiing on the Theodul Glacier in Zermatt, on the Swiss-Italian border. As a passionate skier, I had no doubt my path would lead to the Alps.

One free weekend, I traveled by train to Zermatt. As soon as the magical and historic Glacier Express train pulled out of the station for its journey up the steep Visp Valley toward Zermatt, I was overcome by excitement. I didn't realize it at the time, but the trip would change my life.

The Glacier Express en route to Zermatt

The train was filled with climbers carrying colorful braided ropes, axes, heavy packs and crampons. It was a strange world for me, but it completely captured my imagination. I was a hiker, not a climber, yet I immediately longed to be part of this extraordinary group of hearty souls that scaled treacherous peaks and kept the company of other climbers. I wanted to scale snowcapped mountains and to return and tell the tales. I switched excitedly from one side of the train to the other so as not to miss the soaring peaks capped in eternal snow on both sides of the valley. I especially wanted to see the Matterhorn which I first heard of as a child. My frame of reference was a childhood memory of a ridiculous Bugs Bunny cartoon that featured a climb of the "Schmatterhorn" for the prize of fifty thousand Kronkeits. I'd also visited Disneyland at age fifteen and was fascinated by climbers scaling a miniature replica peak that rose 300 feet above the park while a roller-coaster soared inside the mountain. Disney hired young climbers to climb the different routes on the concrete and steel structure, as mom, dad and the kids watched in awe from below. All these memories from childhood came flooding back even though neither the cartoon nor the ride had much to do with the real mountain.

MEETING THE MATTERHORN

My Mother and I at Disney's Matterhorn, 20 years before my first climb

When I stepped off the train in Zermatt, I immediately gazed up to scan the horizon, eager to see the unmistakable form of the famous Matterhorn. Nothing remotely spectacular was visible through the mists and heavy clouds surrounding the village. It was still early morning, and I checked in to the Bahnhof Hotel, a local hostel favored by mountain climbers and recommended for its inexpensive lodging in a copy of *Let's Go Europe*. The Bahnhof Hotel is owned by the Biner Family, run at that time by the now late Frau Biner. Her brother Bernard Biner, a famous Zermatt mountain guide, was tragically killed on the mountains back in the 1960s. There is a plaque in his honor on the hotel's terrace as a gift to the family from his climbing clients from around the world. It is inscribed as follows "Bernard Biner, a great guide who did so much to help climbers." In fact, Disney chose Bernard Biner as an expert, on-location consultant for its classic 1950s film, *Third Man On the Mountain*. The film documents a young boy's dream of becoming the first person to climb the Matterhorn.

Victory. First Ascent of the Matterhorn (left)
Tragedy on the Matterhorn (Doré) (right)

When I first checked in to the hotel, I was unaware of the Matterhorn's history and so I was particularly captivated by an image of four climbers roped together falling off the Matterhorn. This was a painting by the French artist Gustave Doré depicting the famous first ascent of the Matterhorn by Edward Whymper, in which four of his companions died when their rope broke on the descent. Something about the way Doré painted the snow filled me with an eerie feeling of impending doom. The emotion, my initial impression viewing the Doré depiction, left me with an underlying fear of climbing, and it remained for years.

I shared a crowded bunkroom with many other climbers. Their boots, ropes and gear were strewn about, hanging from the heavy wooden beams of the hotel. I dropped my bag on the bed and quickly headed back outdoors. I am the type of person that doesn't need to see the finish line in order to begin the journey, so clothed only in a t-shirt, shorts and my favorite pair of tennis shoes, I set off to find the mythical Matterhorn.

I followed a rudimentary map in the general direction of the peak. The hike began at the end of Zermatt's main shopping street, the Bahnhofstrasse. I headed up into the foothills, passing tiny hamlets and small chalets, barns and grazing land. Generations of families worked laboriously together storing hay for the upcoming winter or tending to livestock–a stark contrast from the glamorous shops and hotels just minutes away. The hike took me through a beautiful larch pine forest with a glacier-fed stream, unspoiled except for simple signposts showing directions and travel times between various points of interest.

After hiking for about an hour, I reached tree line and the forest disappeared. The trail was lined with scrub vegetation and boulders, and I passed the time daydreaming of the adventures I would have during my summer in Europe. The clouds cleared and suddenly there was the Matterhorn standing before me. I was instantly and forever awestruck by its presence and form. It looms above all, a symmetrical four sided pyramid covered with snow and surrounded by glaciers. The glorious peak stands alone, thrusting skyward, not crowded by other neighboring summits.

THE MATTERHORN IN ALL ITS GLORY

    I doubled my pace to reach the mountain and the longer and farther I trekked, the farther away from me it seemed. I had a map and knew how to follow the signposts, but didn't understand the markings I'd seen for the base of the mountain, for example one that read: STD 5. This was the first time I had encountered these signs and I didn't know what "STD" meant. As time elapsed, I quickly surmised "STD 5" meant that I was still roughly 5 hours from my destination. Even if I'd known this fact, it would not have changed my mind about continuing. I was young, exuberant, fit and highly motivated to get there. I kept hiking, thinking that surely it could only be another hour or so, now that the Matterhorn was in view.

    I foolishly continued without regard for the very real danger of being alone and inadequately clothed against the elements. Zermatt's warm summer day had become much colder and damper at higher altitude, and my exertions had me soaked in sweat. Better-prepared hikers cast odd looks my way as they passed, but I was undeterred and set on touching the mountain.

    Hours later, the terrain rose above treeline and the trail wound its way relentlessly upward through scree fields of loose rock. The trail narrowed and ice and snow appeared in patches. Because of the steepness, the trail zigzagged its way toward the base of the great mountain. In my eagerness to reach the Matterhorn, I cut off as many of these zigzags as possible, feeling adventurous all the while. I sought hand and foot holds to scramble up the sides of the cliffs, noting that my Adidas Stan Smith tennis shoes weren't much good on the icy patches. I clung to the rock cliff with my hands as I attempted to safely negotiate the narrow pathway with its sizeable drops on either side. After five hours at a steady pace and nearly a hundred zigzags up the steep rocky cliff path, I reached snow that sunk in over my ankles. The path became slippery and it would have been quite easy to slip and fall hundreds of feet over rocky precipices.

At the base of the Matterhorn there are two hotels, the Belvedere, for mountain guides and the Hornlihutte, for climbers and high alpine hikers. Hornlihutte serves as the Matterhorn base camp, a lodging place just a stone's throw from the great peak, used by climbers to get an early start in the darkness of morning. Hornlihutte looks like a concrete bunker leftover from the war, completely weather-beaten and long past its heyday, though as I write this a new, modern Hornlihutte is under construction. I walked around the hotel's backside and up a rocky ledge that was covered in slushy snow, stepping in the footprints of climbers who had made the attempt and returned that day. Reaching the wall, I looked up and saw a bronze statue of the Virgin Mary and Child, placed atop the first cliff as a watchful and protective omen.

Hornlihutte Matterhorn Base. Close enough to touch the Magic Peak

I knew immediately that this was a sacred place for me. I was so captivated by the place and mountain that I vowed to come back again someday to climb it. I'd read a newspaper article about climbing the Matterhorn in which the author, who had a particular fascination with the peak, said that he felt a strange energy pass from the rock to his fingertips when he touched the mountain for the first time. He called it the "Magic Mountain," and how right he was. I was hoping to feel a similar electric current, but I did not. I tagged the cliff and started back toward the Bahnhof.

The sun was low in the sky, the temperature had dropped, and a stiff breeze brought snow flurries. The clouds were rolling back in and now I appreciated just how inappropriately geared and dressed I was, and how far I'd have to hike to get back to my hotel. Since I was chilled and wet, time was of the essence. I held a brisk pace over the more than four-hour walk back to Zermatt from the Hornlihutte. I could have taken the cable car and cut two hours off the walk, but I was feeling exuberant after touching my mountain up close. Had the temperatures dropped further, I could have become hypothermic. By the time I reached the village at about 7:30 that evening, I was exhausted and likely delirious. Frau Biner was in disbelief when she learned I had been all the way to the Hornlihutte and back.

In addition to sparking my lifelong love affair with the Matterhorn, that fateful weekend in 1988 planted the seed of an idea for my former business, the Matterhorn Ski Bar. A poster hanging on an old chalet back in the village of Zermatt caught my attention. The headline read "Pizza, Beer, Ski Movies" and advertised a place called the North Wall Bar. The bar was in the basement of an old hotel and hard to find, but when I walked in the door, I discovered people from all over the world drinking big steins of beer, eating pizza and watching Warren Miller films. Two affable climbing bums named Mark and Chris ran the bar. Mark, who bore a strong resemblance to the late actor Patrick Swayze, greeted guests and waited tables. Chris made the pizzas, and was a talented photographer whose work appeared regularly in popular skiing and climbing magazines.

On each visit to Zermatt, I return to the North Wall Bar as if it were an obsessive haunt. The bar's walls are covered with international memorabilia from climbers from all corners of the globe, including a local newspaper story about my own climb which you will soon read about. When I opened the Matterhorn Ski Bar, I framed and proudly displayed the original poster I'd seen hanging on the chalet. In exchange, the North Wall Bar has a Matterhorn Ski Bar menu hanging on its wall.

ROGER AT THE NORTH WALL BAR 1993

2

LAYING A FOUNDATION

Mount Tom

In western Massachusetts, there are hills, a few small mountains and lots of woods and forests. As a child and young adult I would lose myself in the woods near my backyard. Whenever I found life most challenging or I needed to think, I would escape to the woods. Following marked trails or making my own paths, I'd be alone with my dreams and thoughts. I would climb up over rocks and fallen trees and steep escarpments. The challenge and fun was to climb blindly upwards over whatever obstacles presented themselves to discover a new high point. From the top, the panoramas down into the lower valleys, rivers and tree line were visible only to me, from this special secret place where I was the king of my domain. In my imagination I stood atop great summits that none had seen. My escape was temporary to be sure, but one I would return to time and again. Over the years, my dream has led me to a few great summits, and there are a few more on my list for the future.

My dreams began with Mount Tom in Holyoke, Massachusetts. Discovered by Thomas Rowland and Elizur Holyoke in the 1700's, Mount Tom is distinctive and prominent rising just 600 feet above the forests below, yet it can be seen from over twenty miles away. Entering Holyoke from any neighboring town, the mountain is the dominant landmark. As a child running errands with my mother, we often visited the main post office in the center of town. In the marble portico there is a faded mural depicting Thomas and Elizur landing on the banks of the Connecticut River, surrounded by Native Americans of the Pascommuck tribe. In the mural, the natives gaze at Mount Tom, which looms in the near distance. I remember my fascination with the mural and with Mount Tom long before I ever set foot on its trails. Years later, I would explore every acre of Mount Tom and the Mount Tom range, wandering up its flanks and scaling its perilous loose shale cliffs.

Post Office mural with Mount Tom in the distance.

In the 1800's, a grand Summit House adorned the mountaintop, built by the Holyoke Street Railway Company which erected a trolley line to the summit of Mt. Tom. A spectacular fire consumed the first Summit House in 1900. A larger and more elaborate Summit House was subsequently built in the same location, only to burn to the ground in 1929. Constructed as a recreational escape from the heat of the city, the views and cool winds from the Summit House were a popular pastime. Citizens in their Sunday finery would ride the steep rack railway from Holyoke's Mountain Park amusement park hundreds of feet below the summit, to take in the views or socialize near the Summit House on its rocky promontory. Today, a crumbling stone promenade, an iron railing and the ruins of the concrete, supports that once suspended the rack railway, are all that remain of the Summit House and its glorious days. Whenever I return home to Holyoke, Massachusetts, I still climb Mount Tom and run its steep summit trail, training for more adventurous mountain pursuits.

Mount Tom Cliffs

Mount Tom Summit

A TASTE OF THE ALPS

As a senior at Holyoke High School in 1980, my parents sent me to Interlaken, Switzerland with my ski club for a week's skiing holiday during winter vacation. To say that my first real adventure shaped the course of my life would be an understatement. The snow covered Alps of my imagination came alive. Skiing through the deep powder of alpine passes and meadows, I could not believe that this magical world even existed. Pine forests and simple wooden chalets with colorful flower boxes, were overshadowed by giant, majestic peaks.

One day my friends and I were taken to the top of the nearby Schilthorn peak. At the top of the lone mountain was a revolving restaurant made famous as the villain Blofeld's alpine lair in the James Bond thriller

On Her Majesty's Secret Service. A cable car rising thousands of feet in the sky dangles from a thin cable that leads to several mountain stations and ends at the summit. If you descend Schilthorn on skis, the only way down is to follow the trail, or "piste" as it's known in Europe. The descent winds its way around the flank of the Schilthorn, and alternates between steep and more gradual pitches.

Looking out the windows of the cable car, I noticed a lone skier's tracks departing from the relative safety of the normal route. The graceful tracks cut through a narrow couloir between rock cliffs and the snow seemed perfect, knee deep and untouched. For a kid from Western Massachusetts used to skiing the groomed trails on Mount Tom's small ski area, the allure was irresistible.

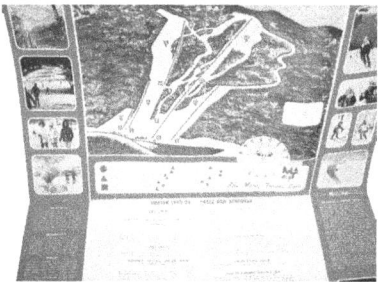

THE SKI AREA ON MOUNT TOM, WHICH UNFORTUNATELY CLOSED IN 1998

I considered myself an expert skier, so thoughts of danger and the thin mountain air did not cross my mind. I challenged my friends, all strong skiers, to join me and follow the lone skier's tracks through the rock bands. From our vantage point in the cable car, this route appeared to rejoin the main piste near the bottom of the mountain. We skied to the edge of the narrow precipice and stared. To me, it looked heavenly, an experience not to miss. I had visions of skiing down the difficult slope and then triumphantly taking a photograph of where my tracks joined the others: a snapshot of adventure, captured forever. Despite my best attempts at coercion, my friends would not follow me. No matter, I would go alone and join them toward the bottom of our run. I jumped in and made large swooping arcs in the fluffy powder, then tightened my turns to negotiate the narrow slot through the rocks. I forgot all about my friends as I lost myself in a skier's reverie. Moments later, I discovered that this path didn't lead back toward the main route. In fact, it didn't lead in any recognizable direction at all. I found myself in the bottom of an immense bowl, too long and too steep to climb and reverse my course.

The only way out was to traverse the flat bottom of the bowl through deep snow to the edge of the next precipice, a vantage point where I'd have a better view. Unfortunately what I saw at that point was that the trail led off the backside of the Schilthorn and away from safety. In the far distance, I could see very tiny impressions of chalets and herdsman's huts in the high meadows far below the mountain. This speck of civilization became my destination; I had to make it there.

I became afraid and realized that if I were to fall and become hurt, I would not be found for a very long time. I skied cautiously downward for about twenty minutes, each anxious minute feeling like an hour. What moments ago had been a marvelous skiing experience was now far from enjoyable. I was terrified, imagining avalanches and deep crevasses – very real possibilities in these mountains. My mind played tricks on me and I visualized my early death. Scared, bleary-eyed and relieved, I eventually skied unscathed into a small village miles away from my friends and the Schilthorn.

On the side of the narrow road leading through the village, a bus stop sign protruded from a snow bank. As I stood next to it wondering what to do next, the local bus pulled up and since it appeared to be heading in the direction from which I came, I got on. The driver and passengers looked at me curiously and had no answer when I asked in English where the bus was going or where I was. I took a seat, looking forlornly out the windows for something I might recognize. Half an hour later, the bus miraculously stopped at the cable car station at the base of the Schilthorn. Enormously relieved, I carried my skis off the bus and got in line for the cable car. I was safe at last and I could not wait to share my experience with my friends. At this point in my life, I began to take pride in doing things that others would or could not do, and I told my story with bravado.

A particular challenge that inspired me was a mountain in the neighborhood of peaks that framed our ski club's daily adventures. It was an ominous and brooding mountain called the Eiger. Its name means *ogre* in German, and the Eiger is steeped in lore and legend. The Eiger's North Face is one of the world's most dangerous and classic climbs. It is a vertical amphitheater in close proximity and perfect view of the hordes of summer tourists and winter skiers that frolic at its base. A battery of telescopes line the hotel balconies below, offering the masses a glimpse of the often deadly escapades as accomplished mountain climbers chase glory. The Eiger is a badge of honor for climbers, and only the bold and most experienced have overcome its perils. On one particular ski trip to it, the community was buzzing with news of an unfortunate climber who perished at the end of a dangling rope on the North Face of the Eiger. To this day, the Eiger remains one of the world's most difficult and dangerous climbs.

As I reflected on this amazing experience, the air, sights and sounds of Switzerland literally took my breath away. It was a disturbing contrast to arrive back in New York City, passing old tenement buildings and the burned out remains of stripped and vandalized cars.

Long after this trip had passed, these famous mountains fueled my imagination, and I dreamed about climbing them. In 1993, I worked for a distributor of European ski products in New York. The company also imported Austrian hiking boots, and I purchased a pair of mountaineering boots. They were more a fashion statement than a practical necessity, but wearing them made me feel as if I was a real climber. I knew I had a long way to go, but I had alpine dreams. I was living in Bedford, New York a tranquil hamlet in the heart of Westchester County's horse pastures. One day after work, I discovered a rocky cliff near the house I rented. It was several hundred feet long and about 60 feet high. The cliff had a variety of routes, and had big handholds so I could climb by scrambling up and over its rocks. It gave me the feeling of climbing something significant, yet did not present any real danger. This cliff became my own east coast Eiger North Face, and I conquered it on a regular basis.

3

THE ALPINE EXPERIENCE

Across Switzerland, the Swiss Alpine Club maintains a network of huts or huttes, each a day's leisurely hike away from one another. Each is staffed by a hut keeper and his family. These high-elevation huts receive supplies regularly from helicopter deliveries and are surprisingly comfortable despite their simplicity. Upon arriving at these huts, one removes his boots and replaces them with a pair of felt slippers. Outside on the terrace, there is always a spectacular view and usually an immense drop below. Tourists take in the sunset which lends the surrounding peaks a pinky-orange hued Alpenglow.

Dinner is served early, promptly at 6 PM and consists of hearty and filling comfort foods like meat, potatoes, or stew. Most huts are decorated in simple mountain décor: black and white photos of climbs, old axes and crampons mounted on the pine walls and sturdy but well-worn wooden tables and chairs. The common bunkrooms are Spartan with mattresses laid side by side in wooden frames. Each climber is issued a pillow and blanket and there is no extra charge for all the late night disruption some climbers make! I've been struck by the wide variety of courtesy among different nationalities in high alpine huts. Certain climbers think nothing of making as much noise as they can and laughing amongst themselves long past lights-out. Climbers turn in early, usually by 8 PM as their climbs require them to rise before dawn at 3 AM. Anxiety rules the night and few climbers get a truly restful night's sleep. Thoughts of the coming adventure are both anxious and exciting, as one never knows what the day will bring.

Climbers must leave the huts by 4 AM to summit before the sun rises high enough to make the climb treacherous. As the sun warms the snow and ice, it turns to a slick and slippery slush that is extremely dangerous and unstable. The objective is to return to the hut no later than noon. This can be especially problematic as climbers without guides have to contend with tricky route-finding, made all the more difficult in the pitch dark of early morning. By the time the sun rises, they have usually retraced their steps many times and lost precious time. There are often areas of loose rock, or old slings and protection which mislead climbers into thinking they are on the correct route. These are just a few of the reasons that the vast majority of climbing fatalities befall climbers who are without guides. One can't overstate the importance of climbing with an alpine guide.

(Protection is any hardware such as vintage pitons or modern day camming devices used to stop a fall…these are usually left behind by climbers in a hurry or caught by bad weather. Slings are narrow pieces of nylon webbing connected at one end to pitons or cams which are attached to cracks in the rock and at the other end to a carabiner in which the climber clips into. If a fall occurs, the climber's rope is secured by the protection and stops the fall.)

Swiss Mountain Guides

Swiss mountain guides share a proud tradition that began in the 1800s. The first guides were hunters and trappers by trade who earned a few extra francs leading travelers across the high mountain passes they knew well. Today many of the guides are third and fourth generation descendants with alpine routes in their DNA. The golden age of mountaineering in the 1860s ushered in the transition to mountain climbing, as local guides learned the most feasible routes to the top of the surrounding peaks. After pioneering climbers conquered the most famous mountains, there was an increased demand for guides to lead others to these summits. Alpine centers such as Zermatt and Chamonix have prospered ever since.

Becoming a Swiss mountain guide is a stringent and highly regulated process. The first hurdle is to become an aspirant guide. Prospective guides (often young climbers) must be recommended by an existing guide to enter the program. Aspirants practice rigorously until they can demonstrate proficiency in climbing techniques on snow, ice, and rock. They need to show competency in evaluating weather evaluation, in anticipating an avalanche and snow conditions, rescue techniques, and a knowledge of first aid. Once the guide-training program is complete, Aspirants serve as apprentice guides for two seasons before being granted their full guide's credentials.

In the early days of guiding, recommendations from satisfied clients were the guide's primary business card. This took the form of an informal guide's book, which contained an evaluation of the guide's credentials and signature from each client. The guide's pride, mountaineering skill, and general demeanor were all scrutinized by his clients and on display in his book for potential clients to see and evaluate. In the early days, there were few clients and many guides so the competition for clients often determined whether a guide and his family had food on the table.

A mountain guide risks his life every time he is hired by a client. Once they are bound together by rope, the guide and client's fates are intertwined. Potential slips by a client must be anticipated and arrested or the guide himself could be pulled down. Guides often test their client's skills before undertaking a major peak, but this is not always the case. Sometimes, a client will hire a guide through the Guide's Office and simply be told on the day before the climb to meet the guide at the hut that evening. The guide will quickly determine the capabilities of the client once the expedition begins. When climbing with a guide, safety comes first. Unlike some ambitious climbers who proceed guideless, a guide will not hesitate to turn back if the weather turns bad, if a client is deemed incapable, or if the route conditions are assessed to be particularly dangerous.

It is generally difficult to develop a personal relationship with a guide. By nature, they are standoffish and private. For the most part they keep clients at a safe distance and fulfill their professional obligations during a climb. In my experience, climbing with a good guide presents a challenge to meet his high expectations and skill. I have climbed with some of the very best guides in Switzerland, and I have been fortunate to develop relationships with two outstanding Swiss mountain guides whose knowledge and charisma helped me overcome my initial fears. No matter how perilous the terrain, I felt as though I would follow my guides off the end of the earth. It was a matter of pride in climbing at their ability, exhibiting skill and developing a bond with a man of honor. I admire my guides, envy their freedom and revel in their company. I have also found that if a guide believes you are a strong and competent climber, he will push you to the absolute limits of your abilities, which can be a very exhilarating experience. Strong guides inspire confidence and fuel your ambition for future challenges.

Historically, there have been far fewer climbing accidents and fatalities among climbers who hire guides. It simply makes sense to employ an expert's knowledge of the route, terrain, snow conditions, weather and history of the mountain. Although guide fees are not inexpensive, what is the price for your life? Paradoxically, many climbers feel hiring a guide would compromise their sport. I still believe that as long as I am climbing the mountain using my own courage, strength and skill, nothing is taken from my adventure if I'm accompanied by a skilled guide.

In Zermatt, the Swiss mountain guides report for duty at the Alpine Center and Ski School, a contemporary glass and wooden building on the Bahnhofstrasse. In the summer, the Guide's Office is a busy place. I usually found a line of tourists waiting to sign up for excursions on the glaciers and up the peaks. The guides evaluate climbers to determine their fitness and potential abilities on the mountains. If a perspective climber is deemed unqualified, the Guide's Office may recommend a better suited excursion. Several visits to the Guide's Office may be required if the peak in question is out of condition or if the weather is unsettled.

Out of condition refers to dangerous climbing conditions: too much recent snowfall on the peak creates a potential for fatal slips, avalanches or overhanging windblown cornices that could release unexpectedly from above.

Climbing with a guide in America is vastly different than in Europe. My first mountaineering experiences all took place in Switzerland, where the guide takes complete and total responsibility for every aspect of the climb. Swiss guides will not even allow you to tie yourself into your own harness. Instead, the guide uncoils his rope, approaches you and ties a bowline around your waist or into your harness. He instructs you every step of the way and is an uncompromising and serious leader. If you make a mistake along the way, the guide will not hesitate to give you a stern reprimand or a warning to snap you back into line.

A guide may "snap you back in line" if you're not obeying the rules of climbing or have lost focus. Mistakes made by inexperienced climbers are commonly caused by daydreaming or a lack of concentration during critical moments. In the States, certified mountain guides allow their clients more independence. Clients are shown the basics and once competence is demonstrated, they are treated more like equal climbers. Clients tie into their own harnesses, coil their own ropes and belay other climbers on pitches. On the descent, European guides keep you on a tight rope as you down climb each pitch until the guide is comfortable with your skills and competence. Being held from above is comforting to inexperienced climbers. But as on most climbs, exposure to severe drops is ever-present. One must still have a head for heights.

When ascending a mountain, a climber faces in toward the mountain. During those early, dark hours of the climb it's important not to see the "exposure" – the sheer drop to the bottom or to a ledge or pitch – seen between a climber's feet. Steep drops can be very intimidating and can cause climbers to panic. It's different on the way down, as climbers descend face out, often looking straight down thousands of feet.

Achieving a summit is a misleading accomplishment since you haven't yet succeeded in completing the climb. You are only halfway there and the safe descent down to base camp is still to come. Most accidents occur on the descent, when climbers are fatigued or lulled by their accomplishment, increasing the potential for a slip.

The proud history of Zermatt guides is marked with a few tragedies. In the 1950s, Swiss National Ski Champion Otto Furrer, a prominent mountain guide, was engaged by a client to traverse the Matterhorn - specifically to ascend the Swiss ridge and descend the Italian ridge. After successfully reaching the summit, Otto Furrer fell to his death on the descent when a heavy fixed rope broke.

In the 1990s, both Hermann Perren and Hans Trachsel were killed when their clients did not heed their critical instruction in particularly dangerous places on the Matterhorn. It is said that upon downclimbing these sections, the clients were told to remain stationary on a ledge and not to move as the guides climbed down to join them at their position. When the rope connecting guide and client comes taut, the slightest movement by the client is enough to pull the guide from his holds. One of the clients did move and both guide and client fell thousands of feet to their deaths. Richard Andenmatten, a guide I've climbed with, was on the Matterhorn at the time that Hermann Perren fell. He actually had to swing his roped client out of the way at the precise moment that he realized a fall from above had occurred. Andenmatten and his client were in the direct path of the fall as Hermann Perren and his client fell. Had they not moved out of the way, they would have been casualties as well. Memorial plaques to both guides are permanently mounted on the Matterhorn and are visible to present day climbers who pass this spot.

In addition to the plaques on the mountains, the cemeteries in the Alpine villages serve as a further reminder of the ever present dangers climbers face. Alpine cemeteries can humble, intimidate and fascinate even the most accomplished climbers. Walking the rows in the Zermatt graveyard, one is filled with a deep sense of history and the pioneering spirit of climbers who came before and perished on the mountains. It is an eerie experience to see stone after stone adorned with a bronzed climber's axe and rope. Gravestones frequently appear in the shape of the mountain on which the climber was killed.

Examples of some of the epitaph inscriptions read as follows:

"I CHOSE TO CLIMB"
"LET ME GO CLIMB THESE VIRGIN SNOWS.
LET ME VENTURE AND HEAVEN KNOWS
GRATEFUL SHALL BE MY QUIET MIND"
"KILLED DESCENDING THE NORTH FACE OF THE MATTERHORN, AGE 23."

I often return to the fascination of the Zermatt churchyard cemetery, wondering if it would be best to visit after my climb. But I am always drawn in. I go to reflect on climbing and on the fallen climbers, many of whom started out on a warm summer day, leaving the villages behind to seek adventure in the hills.

TOMBSTONE IN THE ZERMATT CEMETERY

4

ONWARD AND UPWARD

After finishing graduate school, I moved to Los Angeles. I was living in the city of Glendale in the foothills of the San Gabriel Mountains. There were plenty of trail runs that led to a few small summits, and the amazing views of skyscrapers poking through the smog of downtown L.A. were my preferred reward. Weekends I hiked in the Santa Monica Mountains where the terrain varied from tropical vegetation to arid desert conditions above the tree line. My fitness increased with each hot climb, and I allowed my imagination to run wild, scaling great mental peaks.

My favorite hike led to a sandstone cliff that rose about one hundred feet at an angle approaching 45 degrees. There were some good holds interspersed with small nubbins or dimples in the surface. In certain places, the sandstone would break off in your hand as you tried to reach a hold, making it a committing climb with no protection. A fall likely wouldn't have been fatal, but it surely would have meant broken bones as you tumbled to the bottom. I would scramble to the top trying different routes until I reached a vantage point that looked out over the vast blue Pacific Ocean, again fantasizing of my return someday to the Matterhorn.

SANDSTONE WALL, SANTA MONICA MOUNTAINS, CALIFORNIA 1991

In town, I happened upon a used bookstore with a fairly large selection of adventure and mountaineering titles. I picked up a book titled *Straight Up: The Life and Death of John Harlin* by James Ramsey Ullman. I was hooked at the first page. The story follows the life of the great climber from his early days as a football star and member of the Stanford University Alpine Club to his obsession with Switzerland's notorious Eiger North Face. Harlin was also a man of contradictions. He was an Air Force fighter pilot, a man of conscience and also an aspiring fashion designer. He was a true aesthete. On his most dangerous climbs, he would often stop to admire the beauty of an alpine wild flower. In 1966, Harlin was the first American to climb the Eiger's North Face. His determination to make the climb in the purest way - a difficult vertical climb that followed the most direct line possible and in the dead of winter - ultimately claimed his life when the fixed rope he was ascending snapped.

Inspired by Harlin's story and my own dreams of the Matterhorn, I decided it was time to graduate from hiking to climbing. Adventure 16, an outdoor adventure retailer in West Los Angeles, offered climbing courses at Stony Point, a famous climbing crag in the San Fernando Valley. Stony Point was where famous climbers Royal Robbins and Yvon Chouinard did their early climbing and polished their technique. Adventure 16's course taught the basics of ropes and knots, belay technique (holding falls using a rope and friction device), hand and footwork and the basics of safety.

After my first lessons during which we climbed a few cliffs, I returned to Stony Point every weekend to practice bouldering by myself. Bouldering involves climbing and traversing a large rock that's relatively low to the ground and doing so without ropes, harnesses, or protection. It can be committing if you climb high or without a spotter on the ground to break your fall. Stony Point has two large boulders that offer numerous routes with various levels of climbing difficulty. I polished my climbing technique on several difficult boulder routes, known as *problems* in climber lingo.

One problem in particular gave me a feeling of tremendous accomplishment each time I attempted it. The boulder has a 12-inch hole in its side, about six feet off the ground. On all sides of the hole, the rock is flat without holds. The move requires that the climber place both hands in the top of the hole, performing what is known as an undercling: gripping with the palms up, while moving both feet up the wall under the hole. Next, the climber releases his left hand from the hole and reaches up and to the left about three feet to grip the smooth rolled edge of the rock above. With one hand on the edge, the climber uses the hole as a foothold to gain access to the next pitch, which is then a simple friction climb to the top of the boulder. This particular problem was immensely satisfying to accomplish especially since it was a popular challenge that many could not master. When I first solved the problem, I had to repeat it again and again, each time feeling elation that I had passed a climbing milestone. Once mastered, I could surpass this obstacle almost without thinking, with the same satisfaction each time.

ROGER BOULDERS STONY POINT 1992

For years, I've collected mountaineering books and articles that have taken me to the limits of human achievement, adventure and peril. From classics such as Whymper's *Scrambles Amongst the Alps* and Heinrich Harrer's *The White Spider* to countless newspaper and magazine pieces, each helped stretch my imagination. In the years leading to my first Matterhorn attempt, I had frequent nighttime dreams of my ascent. In them, the mountain always appeared fantasy-like, more like the Disney Matterhorn than the real thing. Sometimes in my dreams, I would nearly reach the summit, but it always eluded me. Yet these dreams fueled my desire and made me even more determined to someday summit the Matterhorn.

The First Attempt

Some climbers collect 4,000-meter peaks like postage stamps. Generally, climbers in America collect Colorado's "14ers" or New Hampshire's White Mountains. Their personal goal is to climb as many as possible and to record their variances and different challenges in a personal journal. Every so often I too feel that undeniable internal need to climb and add to my own collection of 4,000-meter peaks. Sometimes I feel the need to climb to escape the day-to-day trials we all experience. At other times it is to feel vibrant and full of life.

In the motion picture *K2*, one of the protagonists explains to his wife why he would leave her and his newborn son to climb what is perhaps the most dangerous mountain on earth. He tells her, "When it has taken all my courage and all my strength to get there, for one brief moment I feel the truth of my life. I have to have that."

Back in 1988, my very first and unprepared hike to touch the Matterhorn foreshadowed this event." I was unemployed and seeking a career in the ski industry. My long job search had been fruitless, and I felt that if I could just climb the Matterhorn and achieve that one goal, then I could accomplish anything. Weather conditions weren't favorable, and I wasn't yet physically ready or experienced enough for the Matterhorn. I needed to train, yet mentally I craved a significant alpine accomplishment. So once again I traveled to Zermatt.

On my first training hike that trip, I climbed the steep Trift Valley and picked up the Hohbalm route that ultimately led to the Schonbuhlhutte at the base of the Matterhorn's North Face. Joining me were two young American tourists named John and Debbie[1]. Debbie was climbing

---

[1] Many years later, I'd cross paths with John and Debbie again. The couple, visiting Maine for the first time from their home in Cincinnati, came to the Matterhorn Ski Bar for a meal after a day of skiing. Not knowing I had anything to do with the restaurant, they were simply intrigued by its name and our sign with the 3-D relief of the mountain.

without an outer windproof layer, so I loaned her mine. When we finally reached the hut at the base of the North Face, the weather suddenly turned. Chilled after our exertion, we sheltered in the hut to warm up. John and Debbie rested and recharged, yet I was unable to recover. My speech became slurred and I began to shiver despite wearing a wool sweater and many layers. The three of us were all on tight budgets and could not afford to stay over at the hut, considering we'd already booked lodging at the Bahnhof back in town. Although it was a two-hour hike back to the village and I was teetering on the edge of hypothermia, we decided to make a fast break for Zermatt. I found myself in a similar situation much like my first hike back to Zermatt in 1988. We moved quickly, kept each other motivated, and I found the exertion took my chills away. I was fine after a hot shower at the Bahnhof.

[Hypothermia is a condition in which the body loses heat at a greater pace than it can be replaced from exertion. Becoming wet from immersion or sweat cools the body considerably and the cooling increases with wind, cold or dehydration. Depending on the severity and length of time under these conditions, the body begins to shut down and if warmth is not sought quickly, death is possible.]

MILDLY HYPOTHERMIC AT SCHONBUHLHUTTE 1993

The next morning brought more exploration. I'd first visited Zermatt in 1988 as a business student intern living in Milan, Italy. An avid hiker, I was inspired by the true mountain climbers I encountered on the Glacier Express and throughout the village of Zermatt. It was on my first visit that I vowed someday to become a climber and to summit the Matterhorn. On subsequent visits, Zermatt continued to immerse me in mountain

---

What a welcome surprise to be brought together by the Matterhorn yet again, years after our hike together!

culture, in the tragic and triumphant history of the Matterhorn, and in a life I wished to lead.

Zermatt is also interesting in that several families own and control the community, its politics and much of the land and property. Their holdings include many of the finest hotels, as well as the vast network of ski runs and lifts. Bahnhofstrasse - literally translated as *"Station Street"* in German – is the main street that runs from the train station south toward the Matterhorn. Bahnhofstrasse is Switzerland's Fifth Avenue or Champs-Élysées. It's a street of Fancy hotels, expensive jewelry stores selling Rolex watches and lavish diamonds, mixed with sports shops offering skis and climbing gear. Restaurants, tea shops, bakeries and bars enhance the shopping. I dashed in and out of shops buying sports gear, an engraved Swiss Army Knife and anything else that would materially connect me to this magical place. I was thrilled to finally be so close to the Matterhorn and very much in awe of the possibilities.

AN ENCHANTED VILLAGE BENEATH THE MAGIC MOUNTAIN

My shopping gusto foreshadowed buying Austrian climbing boots the following year. As an Aspirant, my purchases made me feel I was nearing my goal. I felt emotionally connected to my pursuit when I owned the gear real climbers used. Looming large in the back of my mind however was sheer apprehension. I was in truth, just plain scared about climbing the Matterhorn. By now my imagination had turned the Matterhorn into Mount Everest. Even the thought of setting off to find a guide intimidated me. I imagined that on arrival at the Guide's Office, that I'd be sized up and deemed unworthy of climbing the magical peak. My fear put obstacle after obstacle in my path.

The standard training exercise to prepare for the Matterhorn is a small rock peak called the Riffelhorn located just off the train at Rotenboden

Station and on the way to the Gornergrat ridge. Climbs on the Riffelhorn closely duplicate the challenges one will encounter on the Matterhorn: exposure, technical difficulty, lengthy rappel pitches and the like, so it is an excellent way for a guide to test a client's ability. I hiked up for a look and told myself that even this smaller peak was way beyond my ability. I feared that my only accomplishment was that I had thoroughly psyched myself out of climbing anything. The mental blocks I was building were getting worse.

The Riffelhorn

Klaus Scherrig and Pollux

Some Brits I'd met at the Bahnhof suggested that Pollux would be a good first climb for me. It would require an ice axe. This seemed exciting and temporarily put my mind off the Matterhorn.

At one of the sports shops on Bahnhofstrasse, I was told there had been an avalanche on Pollux that day. Several climbers had been killed or injured. Immediatly, I began to second-guess my decision to climb Pollux, wondering if I might be getting into something too risky and over my skill level. I decided to get more information at the Guide's Office. I waited in the long line of climbers booking their excursions until it was my turn.

"Everything that could come down the mountain had already come down, so tomorrow will be an excellent day," I was told casually. I had to decide to commit that moment or walk away defeated. I left with instructions to meet my guide and another client at the cable car station the next morning at 7 AM. Three of us would make the climb. As I left the guide's office, I distinctly recall experiencing a somewhat eery feeling and then walking the village in an anxiety ridden, transe-like state which did not leave me.

That night there was no sleep. All I could do was toss with fear of the unknown. I felt as though I was facing a firing squad in the morning.

When I awoke, sheer will helped me resolve that I would climb that mountain and make it back, even if it killed me. (This sounds like a strange contradiction but that's exactly what I said to myself and my feeling was so strong that I remember it as if it just happened.) I now felt empowered and optimistic that this climb would be a defining moment in my life. I was able to alter my mindset and believe that it would be an extraordinary day.

I marched up Bahnhofstrasse as if shot from a cannon to meet my guide Klaus Scherrig. Klaus was a young, 24 year old Zermatt guide who spoke broken English with a German accent. But I understood him well. We waited for the other client who never arrived. So the two of us set off for Pollux. Klaus asked me about my climbing experience. My list of climbs was limited to the Breithorn's South Face a few days prior. The Breithorn, although a good test of stamina at altitude, is technically not challenging by its normal route. Without a guide and in foggy conditions, the Breithorn's greatest danger is hidden crevasses or the possibility of falling in an uncontrolled slide down the steep mountainside.

The cable car arrived at a tunnel that ran through the inside of the Kleine Matterhorn (little Matterhorn) and led outside to the snow. We roped up and started walking across the glacier toward Pollux. I followed, at first filled with lingering trepidation from the night before. Somewhere on that glacier I had an eye-opening revelation that filled me with excitement. As I looked about at the marvelous panorama of peaks, I enjoyed the cool mountain air and brilliant sunshine. It was a day like no other and I calmed down. In the magic of this moment, I realized that my goal was achievable. I had the "right stuff" to achieve it. I recited a familiar prayer, "Though I walk in the valley of darkness, I have no fear, for the Lord is my shepherd…"

I follow Klaus Scherrig across the Theodul Glacier toward Pollux

We came to a narrow snow bridge over a deep crevasse. Klaus lengthened the rope between us to about thirty feet and instructed me to step lightly while crossing. He wrapped the rope around his axe, sunk it into the snow and used this as my belay[2]. I stepped onto the delicate snow bridge and looked down 100 feet into the deep icy green void. Crevasses are chasms in the snow and ice caused by the slow, constant movement of glaciers. Climbers have fallen in crevasses and been found years later, frozen in place, miles from where they were last seen.

Safely across the snow bridge, we continued on until Pollux appeared in the distance. The right flank of the peak had a rocky ridge that connected to an ice field that led to the highest point. It was beautiful with the sun glinting off its snowcapped summit. I was inspired and suddenly I could not wait to reach the peak and begin climbing. When we arrived, we removed some of our extra layers and Klaus shortened the rope. He instructed me to follow his moves and copy his hand and footholds. We went vertically up solid rock with confident hand-holds, reaching a steep section with a fixed chain over an awkward chimney. At this point, I gripped the chain with both hands and pulled myself up hand over hand until I reached a narrow ledge where we stopped to rest. I peered up and saw that a narrow knife-edged, icy ridge led to the summit. Looking very serious, Klaus instructed me to watch every step and not to trip over my crampons. Crampons have a tendency to catch on pant legs or on each other if one isn't experienced in their use.

[2] A belay is the protection of another climber during a dangerous situation. To belay means to safeguard your climbing partner with a rope when ascending, descending or crossing dangerous terrain

KLAUS CLIMBS THE FIXED CHAIN ON POLLUX

The icy ridge was narrow, about three feet wide by one hundred yards long. The ridge had a sheer vertical drop of about 1,000 feet down on both sides. Klaus told me that if I should slip and fall off one side, he would jump off the other side to counterbalance my weight. The rope would save us both. This was not a reassuring thought. The wind picked up and we found our balance difficult as we inched our way up and across the knife-like ridge. I forced confidence and moved determinedly, albeit cautiously. The next thing I knew we had reached the top without dramatic incident. It offered a fantastic panoramic of peaks in every direction. The clouds boiled up and swirled over the mountains in Italy. Klaus joked that the Italians must be cooking a huge pot of spaghetti.

We descended via a different route, at first traversing an ice field and then progressing slowly downward. Klaus instructed me to make sure that all points of my crampons bit into the hard snow and ice with each step for absolute security. By the time we reached the base of the peak and both feet were again on the glacier, my elation was intense. Our climb seemed surreal, but I internalized my feelings and didn't show Klaus. I acted as if this was just another peak I had added to my list. I felt proud even if I wasn't boastful or expressive. On the cable car back to Zermatt, I couldn't help but make eye contact with the ski racers who were on their country's National Team. I felt like a true adventuer. I'd finally climbed my first real peak

Back in town, Klaus and I had a beer on Bahnhofstrasse and I presented him with a Boston Red Sox cap as a gift. Klaus later became a rescue climber for Air Zermatt, the local helicopter rescue outfit. Today he runs an independent guide service climbing peaks from Europe to South America to the Himalayas.

I AM ELATED AFTER ASCENDING POLLUX

RICHARD ANDENMATTEN, THE BREITHORN, AND THE ICE AXE

In 1996, the pull of the Matterhorn was stronger than ever. I was still dreaming about reaching its summit, so I made plans for another trip to Zermatt that August.

Weather in Zermatt can change quickly, making it difficult to plan an alpine trip from the States – especially when using frequent flier miles. Rain in the valley almost always means new snow on the high peaks, and the Matterhorn weather window can be very fickle. Too much snow on the mountain is considered a serious hazard. One too many aspiring Matterhorn climbers have met their end on glazed, unstable rocks, and guides generally do not climb the Matterhorn unless conditions are near perfect. Weather requirements limit the already small window of opportunity

Finally I was able to depart, but on landing, rain streamed down the windows of the plane and pooled on the tarmac of the Zurich airport. It was obvious the weather was not in my favor as I stepped off the plane. The Matterhorn was covered with snow from summit to base, and it was obvious to all that there was too much snow on the mountain for anyone to make a safe attempt.

I wasn't surprised. Just before leaving for Europe, I called the Guide's Office to inquire about weather conditions but was told it wouldn't be safe to climb the Matterhorn for at least another week. One of my favorite books, *The Alpine 4,000m Peaks by the Classic Routes* by Richard Goedeke, offered a comprehensive guide to local alternatives. I devoured it again on the flight. I found the description of the Rimpfischhorn particularly appealing. Goedeke compared its rocky ridge to the back of a prehistoric reptile. The climb, he said, involved a good mix of ice, rock and snow with a few technical challenges and exposure thrown in for good measure. Once again, if I could not climb the Matterhorn, I needed to try something significant. So I arrived in Zermatt having decided to climb the Rimpfischhorn.

The Guide's Office telephoned the Fluealp hut near the base of the peak for a conditions report from the hut keeper. He reported deep snow and no recent climbers, so I was instructed to wait and come back in a few days.

I decided to climb the Breithorn by the normal route for a workout while biding my time until I could tackle the Rimpfischhorn. At the tram station early the next morning, I was shocked to meet my guide who I recognized as one of Zermatt's most famous: Richard Andenmatten. An old videotape in my collection titled *Climbing the Matterhorn* features Richard as one of the guides enlisted to ascend the Matterhorn with a small group of inexperienced climbers. The climbers in the videotape done for a Swiss television show, had been randomly selected for the production celebrating the 125th anniversary of the very first Matterhorn climb. Richard was known as one of the strongest men in Zermatt and also held the distinction of having made the most Matterhorn ascents: over 700 at that point. One of my hopes was to climb with Richard when the day came to attempt my Matterhorn ascent. So I gravitated to him the moment I saw him at the station.

The Breithorn climb is described by some as a monotonous slog, but roped to Richard, I found it thrilling. The climb was straightforward and not particularly challenging, yet I enjoyed it immensely mainly being in the company of a true hero and local legend. It would be like a music fan spending the day with Elvis.

On the tram trip back to Zermatt after the climb, I asked Richard if he knew of anyplace where I could find an old ice axe to display in my restaurant in Maine. He thought for a moment and then generously offered me one of his own. He had used it on many Matterhorn climbs, even rescuing climbers in distress in some cases. Once, Richard had lost it when the axe fell down the Matterhorn's North Face. It was later found and returned to him. Richard considered this ice axe good luck, and I wondered if Richard was serious when he offered it. I thanked Richard and we went our separate ways. I could not get the thought of the axe out of my mind, yet I did not want to get my hopes up. Early the next morning, true to his character, Richard arrived at the Bahnhof Hotel and presented me with this much-treasured gift. He had climbed several hours up to the Hornlihutte at the base of the Matterhorn to get it, and back down again that very day. I was moved by his generosity. The axe was old, well-used and worn, but it was extraordinarily special - almost magical. Frau Paula Biner told me that it is rare for a Zermatt guide to make such a gesture to a client. They are typically friendly but reserved and keep their professional distance from all but a few of their regular clients. I developed a special friendship with Richard and years later, he actually visited the Matterhorn SKI BAR in Maine, presenting me with the gift of a Zermatt village flag. Richard's ice axe hung in a special place of honor on the wall of the Matterhorn SKI BAR along with other special climbing memorabilia and photographs from adventures over the years.

Viktor Imboden and the Rimpfischhorn

A few days later, eager for a significant climb, I returned to the Guide's Office for a new report on the mountain snow conditions. The attendant called up to the Fluealp hut once again, and this time, learned that a party had been up the Rimpfischhorn. I was told to hike up to the Fluealp hut, where later that afternoon I would meet my guide. It was a beautiful blue sky summer day and the hike was pleasant, although long and somewhat steep. I took my time and stopped to take a photograph at the Stellisee, a lake famous for its reflection of the Matterhorn in its deep blue water. After arriving at the Fluealp, I looked fruitlessly for my guide but he was nowhere to be found. A handful of tourists sat outside on the hut's stone terrace, so I ordered a drink and basked in the late afternoon sun. Nobody seemed to know anything about my guide's whereabouts or identity.

FLUEALP HUT WITH RIMPFISCHHORN AND STRAHLHORN PEAKS

Dinner at the Fluealp was served at 6 in the evening; a simple but hearty goulash with hot tea. Partway through the meal, a large, grizzled mountain man appeared in the hut's wooden door frame. I assumed correctly that this was my long awaited guide. Drawing stares from the climbers and without speaking a word to anybody, he got his meal and took it into the kitchen to eat with the hut keeper. True to the guide stereotype, mine stayed to himself and did not eat with me, his client. After everyone finished dinner, the other climbers readied their gear for the morning and started to turn in for the night.

My guide, Viktor Imboden, approached me and in a heavy German accent asked to see my gear. I pulled Richard's battered old ice axe out for Viktor to assess, along with my rented boots and crampons. Everything seemed to satisfy him, and with a nod of approval, I had his blessing to climb. Viktor's face was weather-beaten and deeply tanned. Part of his nose was missing, as was a digit or two on one of his hands. After inspecting my climbing equipment, he told how he'd suffered severe frostbite during a forced bivouac in a storm on Llotse, the Himalayan peak next to Everest. Then Viktor talked of his son who had been an Aspirant guide. The following day would mark the one-year anniversary of his son's death in a climbing accident during guide's certification training. These raw stories of adversity and perseverance were deeply moving and stayed with me throughout the evening. I caught myself wondering what I had gotten myself into with Viktor, and what was in store for our climb the next day.

VIKTOR IMBODEN, MOUNTAIN MAN

Viktor sent me off to get to sleep, promising a 3:00 AM wake up call for our climb. I passed a difficult and restless night, turning Viktor's stories over in my mind and wrestling with my own nerves. Sharply at 3, he knocked on my door. I was dressed and ready to go and joined Viktor downstairs at one of the long wooden tables for a breakfast of tea, jam, and bread before the climb began.

Viktor wore only a cotton T-shirt and pants at the outset of our climb. Despite the early morning cold, he instructed me to remove most of my layers since I would quickly soak them through. The night sky was a deep midnight blue and full of stars as we wound our way up the steep switchbacks above the hut on our way to the snowfields below the Rimpfischhorn. As we rose higher and higher, I continually looked back down to the fading lights from the hut. Viktor's pace was very brisk and I found it difficult to match. I had trained hard for this climb, and at 33, roughly half Viktor's age, I felt humbled by his fitness. Then again, Zermatt mountain guides make their living working at this altitude, climbing several times each week.

We came to the snowline where Viktor roped me up to him. After following a broken trail for about a quarter mile, we reached the edge of a crevasse. Viktor quickly determined that the previous party's route was risky and was too exposed to an avalanche path from above, so he broke a new trail through deep snow. Following Viktor was hard work, yet we continued to climb and posthole up to our knees for what seemed like hours. He stopped briefly for a drink, pulled a little flask from under his neck like a St. Bernard and asked if I'd like a martini. I must have been dreaming from fatigue as he only offered water. He asked how I was doing. Although I told him I was tired, his only reply was, "We go." The Rimpfischhorn never appeared to get any closer and I found myself regretting my ambitions, wishing instead that we were headed back down to the hut, peak be damned.

Then all of a sudden, we were upon it. Looking up from the base was a series of rock chimneys leading up to the clouds. Once again, I had expected to rest before starting up the rocks of the Rimpfischhorn, but Viktor's pace was unforgiving and I was becoming exhausted from our deep snow trek. Viktor instructed me to follow his footsteps and to climb. The rock was solid, but the holds appeared sparse. I watched as the rope moved up the cliffs from him to me, struggling all the while to keep up. If the rope became taut at any point and I slipped, I could pull Viktor down from his holds. I moved more quickly than was prudent and the holds I selected were sometimes marginal or non-existent. I slipped a few times, but somehow found purchase at the last second. By this point, Viktor was out of view atop the next cliff or around a corner, and I could no longer follow his footsteps – I only saw the rope moving upward and had to keep moving before the slack became taut. I was aware that my mind was playing tricks on me. I may have been safeguarded by Viktor from above, but the stories of climbers making mistakes and killing themselves and their guides was in my head and the possibility seemed more real than not. I felt that the next step could be the last.

At the top of the precipice many pitches up the mountain, we came to a steep ice field approaching 45 degrees. We needed crampons for traction and an axe to make upward progress while kicking steps up the ice. This was true mountaineering and I now felt confident and exhilarated. We reached a summit, and I felt sure we were at the top after all that effort. In fact, there were two summits, and we still needed to descend down to a saddle before rising again up steep rocks to the mountain's highest point. A narrow, knife-edge ridge connected the two peaks, demanding utmost caution and focus. And then after all the effort, exhaustion and irrational fear, I took one last step and reached the highest point. At first this moment seemed absolutely surreal, and you might say it was an out of body and mind experience, Atop the summit, all the major peaks of the Alps stood before us and Viktor pointed out each one in several countries. The view was spectacular and in that instant I felt immense pride.

LOWER SUMMIT OF RIMPFISCHHORN FROM THE HIGHEST POINT

Yet, here's the contradiction. For a few minutes at least, I was unmoved. As soon as I reached the top I became dizzy and sat on the nearest rock with my head in my hands. Viktor was elated as we had actually made very good time despite the deep snow. The standard guidebook time is 6-7 hours from the hut and we had summited in less than six in conditions that were far from ideal. Viktor passed me a bottle he had gotten from the hut keeper containing some kind of supercharged Kool-Aid. The sugary drink revived me. We ate a quick bite of dried meat and bread, and then it was time to descend.

Viktor checked the knot in the rope securing me to him and instructed me to be very careful going down. The descent was more difficult than our ascent, as the holds were sometimes out of sight and feel. It required much more concentration. I alternated climbing down sideways and moving like a crab or spider with my back to the wall. Viktor belayed me from above, and I felt the rope tight around my waist. It is easy to assume that reaching the summit means the primary goal has been achieved. But in reality, the climb is only halfway complete at this point. Making it back down is more difficult and tenuous. The dangers are ever-present, yet you are fatigued from the climb. You need all your judgment, strength and complete concentration until you reach the hut once again.

Step after step, downclimbing was tiring and monotonous. We reached the snowfield and retraced our steps. Negotiating the deep snow was just as strenuous as before, but somehow achieving the summit made this effortless. I was relieved when finally I saw the hut appear in the distance, like a beacon on the horizon. We reached the switchbacks where I had watched the fading lights pass from sight many hours earlier, and, as we stepped off the glacial moraine, I could see tourists and climbers alike enjoying the terrace in the warm sun. Civilization and a cup of warm tea beckoned after the day's climb.

Viktor shook my hand and said I was a strong climber. We spoke of other climbs and as I told him my dream was to climb the Matterhorn, he said I could climb the difficult Zmutt Ridge. I couldn't believe it, since I knew the Zmutt Ridge was one of the more technically challenging routes up the mountain. We sat in the kitchen of the hut and ate a hearty bacon stew with fresh apfelstrudel for dessert.

VILLAGE OF ZMUTT WITH THE RIMPFISCHHORN IN THE DISTANCE

For months after Viktor and I parted ways, my thoughts returned to our climb together. It was a strange mix of my own elation and sense of accomplishment, tinged with the memories of Viktor and his living embodiment of the harsh power of the mountains. I realized that on the day of our climb, Viktor was caught up in the depths of his emotions over his lost son. On his solemn anniversary, I was on his rope, along for the ride.

5

THE AUTHOR IN TUCKERMAN'S RAVINE, NH

THE ONLY PEAK THAT MATTERED

Ever since the Rimpfischhorn, I'd held fast to my dream of climbing the Matterhorn. In the spring of 1998, I contacted Richard Andenmatten and made plans to attempt the climb once more. I trained hard in the months leading up to the climb by mountain biking, trail running and lifting weights. I relished any and all physical activity, believing it was strengthening me for my adventure.

Twice a week, I ran up the steep White Heat Trail at Sunday River Ski Resort in Maine where I lived. At the time, White Heat was the steepest, widest, longest trail in the east and its pitch approached 40 degrees. It had a steady, gradual approach of several hundred yards, before steepening considerably and passing over several lengthy boulder fields, then turning to steep flat slabs just short of the top. I ran in my heavy mountaineering boots, which provided ankle support and a more physical workout. Once on top, I'd climb to the top of the chairlift bull wheel and walk one foot in front of the other along its narrow diameter wheel, about 25 feet off the ground. I needed to get used to awkward heights and the exposure I knew I would experience thousands of feet up the Matterhorn. I also climbed the narrow iron rung ladders to the top of the tallest lift towers at the mountain, stopping forty or fifty feet up the tower to stare down the ladder as if I were atop a high dive platform in the circus.

I intensified my training as the time of my departure neared, doing speed hikes up Mount Washington, which is New Hampshire's highest peak and home to the world's worst weather. My record from the Pinkham Notch Base to the Mount Washington summit was two hours and nine minutes along the precipitous, four-mile route. The path winds its way up through the forest, to a glacial circque called Tuckerman's Ravine that has a 50-degree pitch. From there, the route ascends the boulder field of the summit cone to the highest point.

ON A WINTER ASCENT OF MT. WASHINGTON

I planned my Matterhorn climb for July 14, 1998, the anniversary of the first ascent by Edward Whymper and his ill-fated party in 1865 that lost four climbers on the descent. I knew from experience not to plan for favorable weather on a European trip. You can analyze the forecasts, but once you actually land in Switzerland, you deal with what you get. Landing in Zurich, I looked out the window at dark, stormy skies as fat raindrops dripped down the side of the plane. You recall that this had happened before. The weather remained dismal on my train journey south toward Brig, where I would board the Glacier Express for Zermatt. It was easy to think the worst and again fear that I would be unable to realize my dream. After all my years of obsessing, months of dedicated training, and recurring dreams in which I was actually climbing the Matterhorn, I felt I just had to succeed this time.

I got off the Glacier Express to find the Matterhorn shrouded in fog. Zermatt welcomed me with its twinkling lights as I crossed the station square and walked toward the familiar Hotel Bahnhof. Moments after I'd checked in and made my way to my bunk, the desk clerk brought me the phone and said, "It's for you." Surprised, I answered, and the kind, strong voice on the other end said, "See how quickly I get in touch with you!" It was Richard, and I was amazed at his perfect timing. He invited me up to his chalet in Furi, a tiny hamlet just a twenty-minute walk up the hills from Zermatt.

It had been two years since our Breithorn climb, and Richard and I enjoyed catching up. We shared Swiss wine, pasta and dried meat on his outdoor terrace which overlooked the Matterhorn and several other 4,000-meter peaks. I told him I'd trained hard over the past few months and that I felt ready. Moreover, I'd planned some ambitious training climbs in the coming days, including the Oberrothorn and Mettelhorn. Richard told me to take it easy and not to push myself too hard before the Matterhorn. We made plans to climb the Riffelhorn together, the training peak that approximates the Matterhorn's climbing conditions. The Zermatt guides use it to test their client's abilities on rock and their head for heights.

Two days later, I met Richard at the Rotenboden Station, high above Riffelalp at the base of the Riffelhorn. Despite Richard's earlier warning to take it easy, I had felt compelled to hike the two and a half hours up to the Riffelhorn, as opposed to taking the Gornergrat train. I still believed that I needed to acclimatize each day with strenuous hikes. He roped me up and we moved toward the base of the small, steep rock face. I had seen this challenge up close several times, and even though I was a competent rock climber, I was still intimidated by its cliffs. But once we started climbing, I settled into my comfort zone and trusted my ability. I reveled in the challenge ahead. When we were atop the Riffelhorn, Richard's son Robi, a helicopter pilot for Air Zermatt, buzzed over the peak and waved to us from his distinctive chopper with a Swiss flag and red and white stars covering the fuselage. I was inspired and it rekindled my inner drive to be a man of honor who achieved extraordinary goals.

Richard and I climbed several more routes, and just as my confidence reached a high, we tried something altogether different. He had me rappel down about fifty feet to a narrow ledge and then instructed me to climb back up. The holds were few and far between, and those I found seemed the size of a dime. With heavy, inflexible mountaineering boots, it was difficult to find purchase on the polished rock nubs. I managed to climb up a pitch, and then in the blink of an eye, my foot slipped and I peeled off the face. In an instant Richard held my fall without missing a beat and lowered me back down to the ledge. He had me try again and then made me repeat the pitch two more times. I had no further trouble on the Riffelhorn.

Richard told me to meet him two days later up at the Hornlihutte, the base hut below the Matterhorn. I had hoped to climb it on the July 14th anniversary of Whymper's first ascent, but that was not to be. As part of my preparation for the climb, I took a rest day at the Hotel Eden in Zermatt. There was a beautiful indoor pool in the basement of the hotel with Jacuzzi jets and a waterfall, perfect for soothing tired, sore muscles. As I admit now, mine were plenty sore from not heeding Richard's advice and pushing myself hard on training hikes. I wondered if this would cause me troubles later on the Matterhorn. But after spending some time relaxing on one of the solarium's comfortable chaise lounges under the pyramidal glass dome overhead, and flipping through European magazines, my worries were gone. I enjoyed the tranquil garden outside and took in the view of the high alpine peaks, then focused on the Matterhorn challenge that lay ahead.

Two days later, I set out for the Matterhorn. I was entirely confident in Richard, yet still a little unsettled about what was to come. That familiar feeling of intimidation and the unknown was again tugging at my mind. At the edge of the village, a gondola rises up through the alpine meadows passing the hamlets of Winkelmatten, Blatten and Furi on its way to the Schwartzee. The gondola actually passes right over the roof of Richard's chalet, and I stared down at his backyard where just a few days earlier we had shared friendship and a rustic meal. My thoughts were a mix of excitement, fear and anticipation. I had come so far and was on the verge of my obsessive lifetime goal. Would it finally happen?

The Hornlihutte is more than a two-hour hike from the gondola terminus at Schwartzee. Although the Matterhorn appears close when you step off the gondola, it's still quite a distance. The Matterhorn also presents a grand illusion. From Zermatt, the peak looks absolutely impregnable. From the village of Staffelalp below the North Face, it appears to be a big, natural staircase with a modest vertical pitch. From my vantage point in Schwartzee, it now looked easily within reach.

I stopped momentarily at the Schwartzee chapel to pray, find peace and reflect. Local legend has it that the Schwartzee chapel was built by a traveler who got lost in this spot in a blizzard, prayed for salvation and was saved. The trail to the Hornlihutte leads past the chapel, trekking along rough rocky terrain for quite a distance, then up a steep series of cliffs. Once on top, the trail traverses a landscape of boulders and scree before a final climb up a series of zigzag switchbacks. I hiked at a relaxed pace, in no particular hurry and felt that I had earned a leisurely trek to save myself for the ultimate climb. Soon I came upon two hikers moving at a slower pace ahead of me. I passed them and continued on, but noticed that the couple quickly picked up speed and were attempting to pass me. It became an unspoken contest between us to stay in the lead position, and I adjusted my speed in turn. This went on for a while—so much for my leisurely climb! Like many trails in Europe and the Zermatt area, many switchbacks can be bypassed by taking a steeper climb between the turns. I cut off all the switchbacks and arrived at the Hornlihutte after counting 88 zigzags. I was pretty fired up. Call it hubris, but I had once again managed to disregard Richard's advice to take it easy

THE BASE OF THE MATTERHORN

At the Hornlihutte, the deck was filled with hikers hanging out in the bright afternoon sun, drinking beers and using binoculars to stare up the cliffs of the Matterhorn. Richard, who had been silent and pensive in the hut waiting, came outside and we sat together at a weathered table until the sun's last rays fell behind the mountain. The evening ritual is a hearty simple meal around 5 PM, followed by organizing gear, then lights out promptly at 7. It is difficult if not impossible to actually sleep. Bunks are sandwiched side by side with no space in between, and each snoring climber uses just a single blanket and their own clothing or pack for a pillow. I tossed and turned endlessly until about 10:30 when I was awoken by the sound of thunder and raindrops on the tin roof. Surprisingly, I was almost relieved as if the weather meant I would not have to climb in a few hours. Traces of lingering fear remained deep within my psyche.

I awoke at 2:30 and went downstairs to the gathering room to meet Richard. He was pleased to see me up early, so we sat to eat our toast and tea. I drank cup after cup of sweet tea with lots of sugar for energy. The morning arrived clear and cool and Richard's plan on every Matterhorn ascent is to be the first guide with client out the door so he can avoid slower parties and dangerous rockfall kicked down from above.

The Matterhorn is a symmetrical pyramid composed of four faces and ridges. Once above the first cliff our climb began by stepping out onto the East Face. The 50-degree East Face is the side of the mountain just below the crooked overhanging tip of the peak, which looks like a breaking wave. Climbers traverse back and forth across this face for many pitches before returning to the Hornli Ridge just below the Solvayhutte rescue shelter. Most of the climbing of the East Face occurs in complete darkness, with the route illuminated only by the beam of light from your headlamp. I tried to follow Richard's exact steps in the dark, feeling quite afraid of the unknown, of the pitch before me and the increasing exposure below. There are many false paths on this section of the Matterhorn left by unguided climbers seeking the correct route to the top. Many are marked by old fixed ropes or slings still attached to the mountain. Following the wrong path can get you into trouble quickly, as most lead to areas of loose, unstable rock that can break away beneath your feet in a split second. The Matterhorn's constant freeze and thaw cycles disintegrate the rock, and the mountain is literally falling apart one rock at a time. Many deaths on the Matterhorn occur when climbers venture into areas of loose, crumbly rock or get hit from stonefall kicked down on them from above.

Sunrise from the Matterhorn is a spectacular sight. The dark fades to dawn as the day's first light emerges from behind the beautiful Mischabel peaks to the North. The bright rays of the morning sun illuminate the peaks Dom, Taschhorn, Alphubel, Rimpfischhorn and Strahlhorn. As they reach the Matterhorn, the climber is suddenly touched and warmed by the brilliant rays. The experience offers a spiritual and magical dimension to this climb and to being a climber.

Glorious sunrise from the Matterhorn July 16, 1998

From the village of Zermatt and its neighboring hamlets, the Matterhorn's ice covered faces appear precipitously steep. The view is awe-inspiring and is a magnetic draw that attracts millions of tourists to Zermatt every year. The Hornli Ridge, flanked by the East and North Faces with their overhanging ridges. appears incredibly intimidating and impossible to climb. This view discouraged mountaineers from the attempt during the Golden Age of Mountaineering in the 1800s and is the reason why the Matterhorn was the region's last peak to be summited. In reality, the view from Zermatt is an optical illusion. It was not until Edward Whymper hiked to the hamlet of Staffelalp near the base of the North Face in 1865 that climbers understood the mountain's actual profile. From here, the mountain appears to be a huge natural staircase rising at a more modest angle of 45 degrees. It is still to be taken seriously, but it is far from inaccessible.

Once on the Hornli Ridge, the climbing is straightforward with many good holds. There are several more difficult places however, where the guide will belay his client by looping the rope around iron pegs permanently attached to the mountain. Most of the time, guide and climber advance together on a moving belay.

The Solvayhutte, used only for emergency purposes, sits amidst the crux pitches of the Matterhorn climb, nestled into the harsh rock face known as the Moseley Slabs. William Moseley was a young banker from Boston who lost his life in a fall at this place in 1879. Despite and possibly because of the famous accident, Whymper's 1865 climb had inspired others to attempt the Matterhorn, and there were many safe and successful ascents in the late 1800s. Moseley's fall was the first fatality since Whymper's party had perished fourteen years earlier. The Lower Moseley Slab lies below the Solvayhutte, while the Upper Moseley Slab above leads to the shoulder ice field.

Both Moseley Slab pitches are 80 vertical feet, and they are the most dangerous for guides with clients. Richard kept me on a tight rope as I climbed this pitch and instructed me to remain motionless while he climbed to the next stance. Recall that many years ago, Richard's friend and fellow guide Hermann Perren was killed at this perilous point in the climb. Mindful of this, I did not feel even a breath pass my lips and stayed absolutely still while Richard climbed ahead.

We reached the snowfield at the top of the pitch, put on our crampons and looked directly ahead to the Matterhorn's shoulder. This famous feature is a prominent downward slope of snow and ice that juts precariously to the right as an overhanging cliff. At the extreme edge of the shoulder, you can look thousands of feet straight down to the Zmutt glacier below. It is as though you're climbing up an icy church steeple, and you can simultaneously feel both the ground beneath your feet and the edge of your path dropping away, out of sight. Seeing the rock face disappear for thousands of feet beneath you is thrilling but scary.

Crampon climbing is tricky and requires concentration so as not to trip, but the twelve crampon points on each boot make the climbing secure on the steep ice. Richard and I ascended this pitch, and then we looked up at the multi-pitch summit block where the rocky ridge meets the legendary North Face. This is the feature that appears from Zermatt like the crest of a breaking wave. This section of the climb is alternately icy and rocky, necessitating crampons for the icy parts. It is awkward and feels unnatural to climb bare rock with crampons, especially since the scratching sound of the metal points grating on the rock is like nails on a grade school blackboard.

FIXED ROPES BELOW MATTERHORN SUMMIT

Here on the final section of the climb before the summit, there are about six pitches with thick fixed ropes attached to the cliff in 80-foot lengths. This is the site of the first tragedy on the Matterhorn, where Whymper's four companions fell to their deaths. Whymper and his party didn't have the advantage of today's gear, so in lieu of crampons, climbers wore hobnailed boots with nails attached to their soles for grip. Those old fashioned shoes are far inferior to the holding power of ice points on crampons. As legend goes, one climber on Whymper's expedition was inexperienced. At this spot on the mountain, the novice climber slipped from his holds, falling into the Chamonix mountain guide who was leading the descent down these rocks. The impact knocked the guide from his holds and also pulled the next two climbers in succession down in a tragic chain reaction. The remaining three climbers in the party braced for the straining force on the rope. In an instant, the rope snapped, leaving the three stable climbers unharmed, yet horrified as their comrades passed before them down the side of the Matterhorn in a four thousand-foot free fall. A life-size, bronze statue of St. Bernard, the patron saint of mountaineers, now marks the spot of that slip. On this climb, the history of the 1st ascent was ever present in my mind. I thought about it periodically as we ascended, but especially when we reached the spot of the accident.

Close to the summit, Richard pointed out an iron crucifix attached to the rock as a religious omen to keep the Zermatt guides safe. The cross is inscribed with the words *Bergfuhrer Zermatt,* literally translated as *Zermatt Mountain Leader* or *Guide.* Richard was the guide that carried this cross from Zermatt to its final place on this rock.

RICHARD ANDENMATTEN AT THE BERGFUHRER CROSS

Moving up the fixed ropes toward the summit, the weather turned bad. Clouds swallowed the peak, the wind picked up, and sleet pelted our faces. The crampon on my right boot suddenly came loose and hung from my foot, and I had to secure it quickly before it fell off, and I lost it down the mountain. The wind banged my body repeatedly into the rocks, making my task a challenge. Somehow, with one gloved hand gripping the fixed rope precariously and the other in my mouth, I reached down and secured the crampon. Relieved, I continued climbing behind Richard through the deep snow on the final slopes. This was exhausting work, and it seemed to go on forever. To spur myself on I fantasized that I was summiting Everest.

A final 100-yard trudge up steep snow led to our victory. One minute I had been climbing and the next, I had arrived with nowhere higher to climb. The clouds swirled in and out around us, and when they broke, I could see the horizon and thousands of feet down to the glacier below. A light snow fell on the summit, as my ten year dream was finally realized. Overcome with emotion, I simply yelled, "That's Great! That's Great!" over and over until my shouts turned to tears of elation. We had made the summit in 3 hours and 20 minutes, a very good time and well ahead of the five hours it takes the average guided party. I burned the moment into my mind, then regained my composure. Richard took a photo of me with both arms and fists held high overhead in a victorious salute.

THE DEFINING MOMENT OF MY LIFE

Richard asked if I would like to visit the cross on the Italian summit. Large iron crosses are often found on European summits, placed as a protective omen and religious tribute to fallen climbers. Overwhelmed by my summit emotions, I'd forgotten that I'd once set a second goal: to reach the Italian cross.

THE ITALIAN CROSS

The Matterhorn summit is a knife-edge ridge about one hundred yards long, varying in width from about ten to three feet at the narrowest point. It falls away sharply on both sides, dropping thousands of feet to Italy and Switzerland below. It's odd that one can be in such a dangerous place and yet be so inspired by the journey there that the possible peril fades by comparison..We traversed this ridge to the Italian summit, which is on the same ridge but actually ten feet lower than the Swiss summit. At this summit, the arms of the Italian cross spell out the names of the towns on either side of the mountain. *Vallistornench* refers to the Val Tournanche region of Italy and the villages of Breuil and Cervinia at the base of the Matterhorn. *Pratumbori* is for Prato Borni, a name for Zermatt used in medieval times.

I returned to the Swiss summit with Richard to have a quick bite of dried meat, chocolate and a drink of tea. I took photos of the two summits, as well as the view down the mountain of the fixed ropes and the Hornlihutte in the distance. It began to snow, and Richard insisted we start our descent. After dreaming of this moment for ten years, I had spent just ten minutes on top of the Matterhorn. One hundred thirty three years earlier, Edward Whymper described the hour he spent at the summit as "one crowded hour of glorious life." I fully understood his sentiment yet didn't feel cheated by our limited time on top.

Richard checked the knot that attached my harness to his rope one final time, and we retraced our steps back to the first fixed rope leading down the mountain. On his suggestion, I took the descent slowly and concentrated on each step individually. We had climbed the mountain, but of course our expedition was only half way complete and we still had to make it down safely. For much of the descent, climbers face outward and can clearly see the perilous exposure beneath them. Despite this, I felt secure and perfectly safe on Richard's rope. His 700 ascents, intimate knowledge of the mountain and reputation as "King of the Matterhorn" reassured me.

PRAYER TO ST. BERNARD, ON THE 50-DEGREE NORTH FACE OF THE MATTERHORN

We reached the icy shoulder and made sure that each of our crampon points dug deep with each step. Moving at a steady pace, we continued our downward journey to the Moseley Slabs and Solvayhutte. Two roped climbers approached us on their way up and I recognized them as the couple that I raced on the fast paced hike up to the Hornlihutte the day before. When Richard and I hit the Upper and Lower Moseley Slabs, we both rappelled since they are too steep and dangerous to downclimb. It is an exhilarating series of rappels down eighty foot pitches, until the staircase feature on the side of the mountain resumes. Still, we were not without risk. Loose rock, stone fall from above and fatigue persisted as we steadily moved down pitch by pitch. After several hours, the Hornlihutte finally appeared beyond one last cliff, and soon we were grounded, sitting on the terrace.

An Air Zermatt Llama helicopter roared up the valley, disturbing the tranquil post-climb quiet.[3] We heard the loud whop of its rotor blades beating the air furiously as it neared. Kurt Lauber, the keeper of the Hornlihutte and a Swiss mountain guide himself, came outside and conferred with Richard. Kurt is Richard's nephew and once again, I was reminded of the close ties between this small community and its lifeblood, the Matterhorn. A climber had fallen, and Air Zermatt had been called in to retrieve the body.

With the helicopter hovering just above the terrace, a thin steel cable was lowered and a guide clipped the end to Kurt's harness. Seconds later they were airborne, flying up the Matterhorn with Kurt swinging 50 feet below the chopper. The thin cable disappeared from our sight and from where we stood watching in amazement, it seemed he wasn't attached to any lifeline at all. I found a heavy wooden bench outside the Hornlihutte and basked in my summit, yet acutely felt the narrow distance that separates life and death. The helicopter hovered for about twenty minutes before it completed the recovery, roaring again over the cabin on its return down the valley to the Air Zermatt Base and the grim task of identification and notifying the climber's family.

For the rest of the day, my euphoria was tempered somewhat by memories of earlier walks through Zermatt's cemeteries and the afternoon's unexpected accident. Had today's departed climber also walked down the cemetery's rows, contemplating these fallen climbers before he'd set out? Had I inadvertently walked in the footsteps of these Matterhorn ghosts, thinking the same thoughts, fearing the same risks and striving for the same goals they had long ago? I had spent years imagining how I would feel after my ascent and had never once envisioned this blend of eeriness and exhilaration, but the feelings were undeniable.

---

[3] Two years earlier, I'd hired an Air Zermatt crew for a tourist flight around the Matterhorn. Like something from a James Bond movie, I accessed Air Zermatt headquarters by pressing an elevator button on the side of a sheer rock cliff. A metal door opened in the rock face and I stepped inside. The elevator whisks you up through the insides of the cliff, opening at the top to reveal a perfectly level landing pad and series of hangars. Several rescue choppers sit ready on the tarmac outside. The blue and white Air Zermatt

flag with its symbol of the Matterhorn flutters in the stiff breeze outside the Air Zermatt command post.

Eventually, I left the Hornlihutte for the two-hour hike back to the cable car at Schwartzee. I hiked with a teenage climber from the States who had also climbed the Matterhorn. I remembered him from the previous night's dinner at the Hornlihutte. He summited later than I did, and we met in the midst of the chaos at the base during the body recovery operation. Our pace downward was brisk and our steps light. Our hearts were filled with joy and a profound awareness of our accomplishment. In no time, we boarded the cable car back down to Zermatt. Tourists asked us if we had been to the Hornlihutte, and we felt like rock stars as they peppered us with questions once they learned we'd summited the great peak just hours before.

I transferred to a gondola at Furi that took me down the foothills once again over Richard's chalet and to Zermatt. Wandering Bahnhofstrasse back to the hotel, I caught myself daydreaming. The day's events and the moment appeared surreal. The young desk clerk could see it in my eyes as I entered the Bahnhof Hotel, announcing to the whole lobby "We have a summiter under our roof!" The Disney rhyme from childhood flooded my mind… *"When you wish upon a star…"*

The next day, Richard climbed the Matterhorn again with a new client. I hiked up the steep Trift Valley and across the high plateau of the Hohbalm, which offers a fine view of the North Face. With clear weather and armed with a set of binoculars, I scanned the peak for signs of Richard and his climber both on the ridge and on the shoulder, to no avail. I continued down past the village of Zmutt to Staffelalp, looking straight out at the Hornli Ridge's profile and the perpendicular vertical cliffs of the North Face. From this vantage point, I clearly saw why generations of would-be climbers were fooled by the peak's illusion of impossibility. It was somewhat surreal to realize as I gazed up at the Matterhorn repeatedly, that just 24 hours before I had climbed to its summit and back.

I returned for my last night at the Bahnhof feeling fresh from my day's adventure. As I passed through the lobby, Frau Biner's niece suggested I should run marathons next. Indeed, this was perhaps the fittest in mind, body and spirit I had ever been. Richard invited me back to his chalet for dinner that night and we sat outside on his terrace. As the sun faded across the great peaks, we toasted the Matterhorn one more time.

6

I FIND MY LIMITS

In early 2000, my life was unsettled. A painful personal issue made my heart heavy, so once more I turned to the Alps for comfort. The call of the peaks was stronger than ever, urging me to climb again and clear my head. I called Richard Andenmatten about planning an August trip, but he was unavailable. He referred me instead to a young guide named Helmut Lerjen. Helmut was from the village of Tasch just north of Zermatt. Our meeting would prove to be fortuitous, and I would be taken to the absolute edge and beyond.

Helmut was friendly, skilled, and a bold guide who tested my limits fully. He spoke in a thick German accent and was always fun loving and quick to laugh. He was also very contemplative and logical. As a guide, he had participated in numerous alpine rescues and demonstrated a selfless character and deep respect for his craft.

I had all sorts of ambitious plans for this trip, I wanted to climb the magnificent Weisshorn, the Taschhorn, or the Obergabelhorn, all 4,000-meter peaks that loomed high above Zermatt. Helmut and I first met in Zermatt at Grampy's Bar on Bahnhofstrasse to put together the itinerary for our week of climbing. Grampy's reminded me of those trendy restaurants in New York or Boston with French doors that open up onto the street. We had a beer and took in the people watching as an unending parade of tourists and climbers passed. Once again, conditions were dangerous with too much snow on many of the peaks I'd hoped to climb. Richard had informed Helmut that I was a strong client, so our plan included four days of climbs chosen to push me to my limits. Between Helmut's easy smile, likable demeanor, and thoughtful planning, I felt confident it would be a challenging week. In retrospect, it was much more.

HELMUT LERJEN AND BREITHORN NORTH FACE

DAY ONE: LEITERSPITZEN

We began with a peak called Leiterspitzen just above the village of Taschalp. Although the Leiterspitzen's summit falls just short of being a true 4,000-meter peak, it was every bit of a challenge to me. I met Helmut early on the morning of our climb just outside Zermatt. He drove us through Tasch, and above the tree line to Taschalp where the climb began. We hiked for about an hour to reach the start of the climb, which was a zigzag traverse up scree slopes to steep rock that we had to scramble. "Scrambling" is negotiating steep terrain with hands and feet and usually does not require ropes or protection. This particular morning was chilly and the rocks lower down on the Leiterspitzen were glazed with a thin film of ice, known as verglas. It was somewhat dangerous to climb these rocks before the sun had sufficiently melted away the ice. I was nervous about the climb, but kept my fears to myself and followed Helmut.

The Leiterspitzen ridge is made up of a series of eight or ten rocky pinnacles that jut up like minarets thirty or forty feet high on the way to the summit. I had thought it odd that Helmut told me to bring along my rock climbing shoes on this peak, but the reason was apparent as we made it to the long jagged ridge that is the crux of this climb. One after another, we scaled each pinnacle up one side and down the other. The climbing was exacting and I needed every bit of the rock skills I'd acquired over the years. Each hand and foothold was like a move in a game of chess, forcing me to anticipate several moves ahead. As we climbed higher, there was a magnificent bird's-eye view of Zermatt far down in the valley with the Matterhorn off in the distance. Helmut and I took photos of each other on top of these pinnacles. My favorite is of Helmut straddling one of the minarets with a significant drop down all sides.

LEITERSPITZEN PINNACLES AND LEITERSPITZEN SUMMIT

Soon, the summit was in sight. A light snow covered the rocks leading to the highest point. As is traditional atop many alpine peaks, an iron cross with an attached climber's log marked the summit. I added a personal message to a girl back home and signed my name and the date of our climb.

Summit Leiterspitzen

Atop the summit, Helmut and I shook hands and shared a quick snack. Two other climbing parties we'd encountered on our ascent arrived, and Helmut recognized them as two Aspirant guides practicing their soon-to-be profession with friends. After taking in the view, we all set off down the mountain by a different route. At the first cliff, Helmut set up a belay for a rappel, and one by one, we abseiled 100 or so feet down the pitch. Several additional long rappel pitches followed until we reached the scree slopes at the base of Leiterspitzen.

After our climb, Helmut introduced me to his friend Gabriel (Gabi) Willisch, another local guide. Gabi had a long white beard, bore a strange resemblance to St. Nick and lived alone in a small chalet high in the Alps. The chalet's interior was rustic and the walls were decorated with stuffed animal heads that Gabi had hunted including ibexes, marmots, chamois and small rodents that looked like saber-toothed squirrels. Gabi was a colorful character and told stories of his climbing exploits throughout the decades. We enjoyed his company (and a few beers) as we watched the sun set on a pristine alpine day.

That night, I had been invited to Richard's chalet to celebrate his son Robi Andenmatten's birthday. A tent was set up in Richard's yard, and many guides and their families were there for the party. The guide group is a close community, like a fraternity colonized in the shadow of the Matterhorn. Richard's nephew Kurt Lauber, whom I remembered from his role in the body recovery on the Matterhorn two years earlier, was there with his family. I had been inspired by his demeanor that day and looked to him as a model for how I wanted to be: resolute, courageous, and defiant. I was proud to be in the company of these men.

Robi, a lead helicopter pilot for Air Zermatt, helped train Himalayan pilots in high alpine rescue techniques in the Everest region. He made a grand entrance at the party, landing his Llama helicopter on Richard's lawn - something that would never happen in America! A short while later, an emergency call came in and the crew jumped into the chopper and flew off in the direction of the Breithorn. A snowboarder had gone missing on a glacier earlier in the day. The rescue was successful, finding the snowboarder in a crevasse and delivering him back to safety. Before I knew it, Robi and his crew landed the chopper on the lawn a second time and rejoined the party.

AIR ZERMATT ARRIVES AT THE PARTY, ROBI READY TO BBQ.

ROGER AND THE HEROES OF AIR ZERMATT RESCUE

Day Two: The Breithorn Traverse

The next day, Helmut and I were off again early, set to conquer the Breithorn Traverse. This time we met at the gondola station at the edge of the village and rode up to the tram, ultimately arriving at the Kleine Matterhorn, which is the starting point for summer skiing or climbs. Kleine translates to "little" in German, which is appropriate for this small jagged peak above the Theodul Glacier. It looks like a miniature Matterhorn. From there, Helmut roped me up and we traversed the Plateau Rosa for about an hour. The Plateau Rosa on the Swiss/Italian border is a glacier that leads beneath the Breithorn Massif toward the 4,000-meter peaks Castor, Pollux, Lyskamm and Monte Rosa, Switzerland's highest peak. When we reached the end of the Breithorn, we started the vertical climb. Helmut's plan was to traverse the Breithorn ridge back to the summit, which he said would be an interesting climb. It turned out to be far more than that.

The Breithorn's normal route is the easiest 4,000-meter peak in the Alps, and is highly recommended as a first excursion for those who aspire to become climbers. The Zermatt guides use it to test clients' stamina and dexterity with crampons. The Breithorn is not far from the Kleine Matterhorn, and its normal route is simply a long and strenuous snow slope that leads to a magnificent view of peaks, glaciers and Zermatt far below. On beautiful summer days, the Breithorn summit will seem like a picnic with hordes of people taking in this lofty promontory. Helmut, however, steered us off the normal route and onto an alternate course. Our traverse was a narrow knife-edge ridge about a mile long, with a two thousand foot vertical drop down each side. At times, precarious, windblown cornices appeared which required delicate steps in just the right places to avoid falling to the glacier below. Helmut climbed up cliffs that reminded me of the famous "Hilary Step" on Everest, which is a slightly technical 40 foot cliff made difficult by the thin air of extreme altitude. Here, it was not so much the added difficulty of the altitude, but rather the immense drops down either side which added challenge and made you concentrate on each step.

BREITHORN TRAVERSE AND HELMUT SCALING CLIFFS ON ROUTE TO THE SUMMIT

On this climb, Helmut shared his rope knowledge and guiding tips, teaching me a few things that would prove useful in my future mountaineering experiences, such as how to tie a "prusik knot." A prusik is a knot that can be tied to the main climbing rope that binds it when under stress or load. The knot can be useful as a backup belay to provide extra safety in a rappel or rescue situation.

Off in the distance, an Air Zermatt helicopter hovered over the Breithorn's summit and North Face. Climbers, most of which had come up the normal route to the top of the Breithorn, looked like small ants, barely visible from where we stood. Within an hour we joined the party on the summit, and quickly continued back down to the Kleine Matterhorn to take the tram back to Zermatt. The Breithorn Traverse had been one of my most challenging climbs to date.

Day Three: The Riffelhorn

Helmut's plan for our third day included a series of climbs on the Riffelhorn, which was familiar to me from my training climb with Richard. The jagged rock peak is short, but some of its pitches nearly duplicate climbing the Matterhorn, making it ideal for Matterhorn hopefuls.

At the Riffelhorn's base, Helmut looked up toward the Matterhorn with binoculars and noticed a solo climber on the shoulder ice field. He sensed that the climber would have trouble, since it was fairly late in the morning and the bright sun was warming the snow into unstable slush. Helmut and I quickly reached the top of the Riffelhorn, and pushed on toward our objective for the day. We rappelled down the South side where the climbs are more challenging. Just below us, an amazing blue-green pool of glacier-fed water appeared as an oasis on the barren moraine. It was a hot summer day and I fantasized about dropping off the cliff into the pool, but quickly thought better of the idea.

The "Kantethermometer" route above us was fairly new, with bolts attached by Helmut's friends for lead climbing. This was their alpine playground, and when they weren't guiding paying clients on the high peaks, they climbed here together for sport. This route offered some of the hardest rock climbing I've ever done, requiring extreme concentration and steady hands and feet on minuscule holds. It was incredibly satisfying to climb these pitches well.

Zermatt guides carry emergency radios linked to Air Zermatt and a report came in on Helmut's that a climber had fallen on the Matterhorn. We looked up, scanning the mountain for the climber we had seen earlier but could only see tracks in the snow on the shoulder. We later found out that Air Zermatt had recovered a young Dutch climber's body. My heart went out to this adventurous climber, and I was shaken by the realization that I had been one of the last people to see him alive.

At the day's end, Helmut and I went once again to Grampy's Bar, to plan our final day which would be the most challenging expedition yet.. After a beer, Helmut left to borrow a pair of ice tools or axes that I would need for our Breithorn North Face attempt.

Day Four: Breithorn North Face

We met the next morning at the Gondola station. Our objective was the Gandegg Hutte. The hut lay on the rocky moraine below the Breithorn North Face. It was especially rustic and reminded me of a small Siberian military outpost, yet it was home for the afternoon and evening. Helmut and I sat outside on the terrace in our slippers, and I felt a now familiar feeling: a twinge of real fear as I looked up and scanned the North Face with binoculars. I'd had very little experience climbing steep ice with tools and this face looked beyond what I thought I could handle. Yet I was committed and surrounded by climbers who were discussing their North Face plans. I ate my meal that night as if it were the last supper. Even though I now had mountaineering experience, I'd felt this way before Pollux, on the Rimpfischhorn, and also the Matterhorn. Perhaps this was normal since climbing is always a calculated risk, even with a competent guide. I trusted Helmut and felt comfortable with him.

Breithorn's North Face

When I awoke the next morning I felt a little off, but I couldn't explain it. We started out the door at 3 AM and traversed the Breithorn glacier for an hour before reaching the bergschrund at the mountain's base. Bergshrunds are crevasses that separate a glacier from the peak. Helmut found a snow bridge to cross and soon we were climbing up the lower flanks of the Breithorn. I was still groggy from my listless sleep. The climbing became steep and required three solid points of contact with axes and crampons. Helmut and I encountered a steep jumble of huge ice blocks on the hanging glacier called seracs that form from the constant pileup of ice moving downhill. The ice creaks constantly from slight movement and can release without warning. So moving quickly is prudent. In my haste, I suddenly slipped and fell about ten feet before Helmut arrested me and stopped my fall. I still don't know if or how he anticipated my slip, but he was able to prevent a long dangerous tumble for both of us. For the second time in four days, I'd climbed rocks covered in verglas, unable to get solid axe or foot placement. Verglas forms when water flowing over the rock freezes to a fine film. It is nearly impossible to see in the dark. My crampons would not bite into the rock, and I fell. The fall woke me up like a cold shower. The experience stayed with me and foreshadowed the climb ahead. Helmut and I continued on, but my confidence was shaken and my steps were tentative. I regained composure after a while as we traversed left, up a steep couloir that led to a steep, 60-degree ice field.

Several pitches later we came upon unsecure ice again. I struck the mountain with my axes repeatedly and finally got them to stick after many blows, but they did not feel secure. I kicked my crampon points in to the mountain but they skidded or bounced off the icy rock. Frightened, I called out to Helmut that I was in trouble. Seconds felt like minutes as I watched him wind in an ice screw to secure us. I waited, praying for him to clip in a carabiner. My legs trembled like a sewing machine as I imagined myself peeling off the side of the mountain. In an instant, Helmut clipped in and we were safe. He held me fast until I found new and more secure placements. The peril had passed but my unease about wanting to survive and to summit dominated my thoughts.

We continued for several more pitches until we got to the rock bands just below the summit. Here the ice was secure, mirroring the 60 degree couloir we had ascended hours earlier. My confidence returned and soon we neared the summit. Compared with the drama of the ascent, coming over the top of the North Face and joining the masses who had ascended the normal route was almost anticlimactic. As Helmut and I stepped above the dangerous ice wall onto safe ground, the others stared at us as if we had just come from the moon.

I'd earned a brief stop for a victory photo with my axe in the air and then we descended to the Kleine Matterhorn tram station. I pushed myself to the absolute limits of my ability and a bit beyond, and I was humbled. Simultaneously, I felt elation, pride, and satisfaction. My thoughts then returned to my troubles on the North Face and with Helmut. It was left unspoken as if he was aware and in complete control of our fate, even though to me I was in a near death situation. He treated me as a friend, an equal, who shared extraordinary life challenges. I recalled all the tragedies I'd witnessed climbing these peaks, knowing some of those mountaineers were far more competent than I and once again I was keenly aware of this fine line.

We took the tram back down as far as Gandegg, and I got a rush of adrenaline, feeling fitter than I ever had before. I looked back up at the Breithorn North Face and nearly burst out of my skin. I was a superhero in my own comic book.

Summit Victory: Breithorn North Face.
The Matterhorn in the background

It had been an intense week of climbing. The following day, I met Helmut at the train station in Tasch for a last beer and to settle up his fees. It had been a lucrative week for Helmut: 2,220 Swiss francs total, 800 of which were for the Breithorn North Face alone. He had earned his fee. In his thick accent, Helmut told me that I was a strong client and asked if I would be back again the next year. I said I hoped to do so, but I also couldn't imagine how to follow up this epic trip with anything grander.

I left Zermatt and landed in Boston the following day, prepared for the jolt back to reality. My reentry was complicated by the fact that the airline lost my luggage. I had packed a North Face mountain guide parka, rock shoes, a harness, carabiners, and the other assorted gear I had used in Zermatt. Unlike the usual hassle when a bag is lost, then found in a day or two and delivered to your home, my luggage appeared to have vanished. Weeks went by and the airline finally told me to replace the things I'd lost and submit a bill.

As I'd told Helmut, I had every intention of returning to Zermatt the following year, but fate intervened. I broke my leg and blew out the Anterior Cruciate Ligament in my knee in a skiing accident several months before my planned return. I'd had a few surgeries, so when I did come back to Zermatt the following year in 2001, I was not climbing.

I was not done with mountaineering but the hiatus caused by my accident did me good. I was unable to climb but instead I had precious time to reflect and enjoy the scene without the constant sense of urgency to get up into the mountains and achieve summits.

7

CLIMBING CLOSE TO HOME

THE GUNKS

In the fall of 2000, I was casually dating a climber. I'd just returned from my Alps adventure with Helmut and she suggested that we should visit the Shawangunks in New Paltz, New York. This huge climbing mecca just south of Albany is commonly known as the Gunks, and its striation and geological composition give it a reputation for offering absolute solid rock and an abundance of tricky holds. The climbs are steep and committing with lots of exposure, and the highlights are the incredible holds that stretch climbers physically and mentally. You can feel for them with your eyes closed and the climb inspires tremendous confidence. Many of the holds are "Thank God" holds, meaning they're huge and solid enough to allow climbers to hang off a vertical cliff hundreds of feet above the ground with no fear of slipping. I get a natural high when I climb well in exposed places, suspended from a cliff high up on a pitch, looking around and listening to the silence. In those moments, time stands still for me. It is a pure experience that cannot be duplicated. I can be scared to death, yet feel in complete control at the same time, which to me is the definition of adventure.

The Gunks are historic and legendary stories are told about the exploits of a merry band of pranksters known as the Vulgarians. A charter member of this group established most of the climbing routes in the 1950s, and later went on to found a climbing shop called Rock and Ice in New Paltz. Members of the Vulgarians were known to climb nude at times, and had a reputation for outrageous drunken revelry beside burning campfires in the Gunks. Since I needed all new gear, we visited Rock and Ice and I purchased a new harness, shoes, carabiners, and all the rest of the items I'd lost to the airline. My girlfriend and I camped with some climbing friends of hers from Maine, and did several routes that weekend. I was second on the rope, as I do not trust my life or anyone else's to my skills as a lead climber.

Cathedral Ledge

A few weeks later we were in North Conway, New Hampshire climbing Cathedral Ledge. The most popular route, known as "Thin Air," is rated a solid 5.7. The American rating system for climbs starts at 5.6 and involves rock scrambling using hands and feet in unexposed places. A rope or protection is not needed. The top of the range and the absolute limit to what is possible is 5.14. My ability at the time was a pretty solid 5.8 – 5.9. The Thin Air route is a multi-pitch, lead climb that zigzags up a vertical ledge for several hundred feet. At the top of Thin Air is a broad ledge which is the end of the climb for most. One of the most challenging climbs at Cathedral begins from this ledge just above Thin Air and is known as Pine Tree Eliminate, rated 5.9 on the classic scale. This route is a classic crack climb, finishing at a pine tree that grows out of the crack at the top. My lead-climbing girlfriend decided we should try it, and fresh from the North Face of the Breithorn, I was game for anything. She was a strong climber and I trusted her, making us a good climbing pair.

The first move requires a lunge to the first hold and is really tricky, especially for short, vertically challenged climbers. I watched as she grabbed this hold and then pulled herself up into the crack. With a delicate hand jam, she quickly attempted to put in a piece of protection. She was about seven or eight feet above the deck at this point and was having trouble finding a placement for the pro. She became anxious and started having the same sewing machine trembles I'd had on the Breithorn. I was afraid she was going to peel at any moment. This first move is one of two crux moves on Pine Tree, and is the more difficult of the two. Understandably, she didn't want to peel since she'd land on the solid ledge and likely break a bone or two in the process. She was on the verge of losing her strength and almost her composure, when at last she succeeded in inserting a wire nut and clipping in. With several more delicate moves she was on top, ready to belay me up. Since I'm tall, I got the first move without too much trouble, but it was sketchy and I could see why it was considered a crux. It was all crack, all the way up. Negotiating it required a series of hand jams, foot jams, underclings and a few other tricks from the toolbox. I found the second crux more difficult and it took me a while to overcome. The move was an overhang, requiring delicate hand holds and proper foot placement, leaning out and almost backwards. The overhang must be mantled, but the reward for mastering it is the Pine Tree. I was stunned to realize this climb was as hard as the Breithorn, albeit just a single pitch!

That winter, I met my future wife, Thea, at the Matterhorn Ski Bar. She was a skier, but not yet a climber. It was on a warm spring skiing day at the end of the season that I had my skiing accident, broke my leg in two places, and blew out the ACL in my knee. I was skiing with a group of friends and after many runs, they decided to call it quits and hit the sun deck of the lodge for a beer. But I just couldn't get enough of the day or the skiing and went up for one more run.

There was a jump close to the deck but a little closer to an iron stanchion that held a barrier fence. I came down the inrun with too much speed and a little too far to the right to negotiate the jump. As I attempted to correct my course, the soft sticky spring snow grabbed my skis, stopped me in my tracks, and threw me into an out of control tumble straight into the stanchion at about 30 miles per hour. The iron pole caught my right leg just above the ski boot, instantly breaking my tibia and fibula. I lay on the snow in full view of my friends on the deck before going into shock. I knew I had broken bones.

We had planned a European trip for that summer, which of course included a visit to Zermatt. But as both Richard and Helmut were away, and as I was unable to climb, it made for an odd visit. Still, Thea and I hiked up to the Riffelhorn and sat by the Riffelsee. The reflection of the Matterhorn was unchanged. I stared up at the summits that I had reached and was at peace without needing to climb.

Back in the states that fall, Thea and I hired a guide to climb Thin Air on Cathedral Ledge. Thea had natural ability and was not afraid of heights. Although she enjoyed the climb, it wasn't particularly significant to her. Her enthusiasm for climbing didn't match my unbridled passion.

We also top-roped a few times at our local crag, Tumbledown. Again, Thea impressed me with her abilities on some tricky routes. I hadn't climbed anything significant in quite a while and I began feeling that old pull. This time I daydreamed of introducing Thea to the Alps too.

CATHEDRAL LEDGE NEW HAMPSHIRE

THE GRAND TETON

The peak in the continental U.S. that's most similar to the Matterhorn is the Grand Teton in Teton National Park, Wyoming. At 13,770 feet, it is roughly 1,000 feet lower than the Matterhorn, but the two climbs are similar in many ways. In the summer of 2002, that inner voice was calling me to climb a peak again. I had been intrigued with the Grand, and began making plans for a climb with an old high school friend. When the friend backed out, Thea offered to come instead. She was excited about the trip and took the climb seriously.

I researched the peak and learned that the classic route was the Exum Ridge, named for Glenn Exum who made the first ascent in 1931. He did it wearing football cleats for climbing shoes. Exum later went on to found Exum Mountain Guides with fellow climber Paul Petzoldt, who himself had founded the National Outdoor Leadership School (NOLS). Today, Exum is the world-renowned standard for guide services and some very famous, elite climbers are Exum guides. The late Alex Lowe was an Exum guide, and considered one of America's greatest climbers prior to his premature death in an avalanche on Shishipangma in the Himalayas. Guides do not apply to be accepted by Exum. They are invited by the world's elite climbers or sponsored by other Exum guides. Only the best of the best can call themselves members of the Exum fraternity.

In preparation for our trip, I registered Thea and myself for climbing school, a prerequisite for all but the most highly skilled, world-class climbers. The school is Exum's way of maintaining safety. It provides the Exum guide with the absolute surety of the climber's basic competence on a high mountain peak. Thea and I flew into Jackson Airport in early September, the final seasonal window for climbing the Grand. The weather appeared fine. As the plane came in for final approach, we passed the Teton Range up close, with the Grand featured prominently on the skyline. It was spectacular in its own way, but not comparable to the drama and majesty of the Matterhorn. We settled into a condo in Teton Village. Our balcony looked out over an unspoiled, wild west scene that included horses in the valley, mist floating up over the sagebrush, and hot air balloons floating effortlessly on thermals. It was dreamlike, but I was focused on climbing the Grand and would not be distracted. We were there for a purpose, and all the beauty in the world would not put me at peace if I wasn't able to climb.

The Teton Range

Thea and I set out to explore the area. Moose, Wyoming is one of the highest per capita income areas in the United States although it doesn't look it at first glance. The Tetons are the majestic backdrop for world-class fly-fishing, horsemanship and serious wine collecting. We found a wine shop selling $500 bottles of vintage wines, and noticed grand log home mansions with seven figure price tags in neighborhood after neighborhood. Our favorite local hangout, Dornan's, was a rustic place with a roof deck with a breathtaking view of the Teton Range. It was the perfect spot for a flatbread pizza and cocktails after the intense sessions at the climbing school.

Early the next morning, we took in a hike for some acclimatization and fitness. Thea and I rode the famous Jackson Hole tram to the summit of Rendezvous Peak and caught a different glimpse of the Grand from a new vantage point. The hike took us into Cody Bowl where we got off trail and had to bushwhack our way down. It was a strenuous but enjoyable hike, and we were vigilant about watching for aggressive bears that inhabit the Tetons. We'd timed our excursion to avoid the late afternoon lightning storms which can be a frequent and a dangerous occurrence in the late summer and early fall. In fact I'd picked up the local paper in town and read a story of three guideless climbers who had perished on the Grand after they got caught in a lightning storm on the previous day. Climbing of course meant risk, but the newspaper piece added the familiar dose of intimidation I so often felt before a big climb.

ROGER AND THEA IN CODY BOWL

The first day of climbing school began with a briefing at Exum HQ, a rustic log cabin that appeared to be the original from the days of Glenn Exum. We arrived, equipped with the requisite special climbing shoes that were a combination approach shoe and rock shoe with a flexible sticky rubber sole. We broke into small groups and were assigned a guide. Like all Exum guides, our leader Tom Schiolino had a solid gold climbing resume. He was serious about his craft, yet lighthearted and a regular guy.

Thea and I took to his demeanor immediately and hoped that he would lead us up the Grand in a few days.

Across the parking lot and on the other side of Jenny Lake was Cascade Canyon, where we practiced basic climbing skills in a perfect crag amphitheater ideal for training. Everyone was exposed to knot tying, belay techniques and fundamental climbing moves such as underclings, smearing, and edging. We had a chance to boulder a bit, belay each other, and get the feel of rock climbing on a short, manageable climb. This was a perfect introduction to the climbing world for hikers who wanted to take the next step.

Day two was more intensive with multi-pitch climbs, numerous belays, and rappelling. The final rappel was about 80 feet and simulated the descent of the Owen Spalding route on the Grand which requires a 120 foot rappel to get back down. I was particularly proud of Thea, who showed poise, grace, and agility in mastering the concepts. I found the class to be fun, but then again, I find any chance to be on a rock fun.

THEA ROCKS IN CLIMBING SCHOOL, SEPTEMBER 2002

Those of us deemed acceptable were placed in groups of three and paired with guides for our challenge on the Grand. Unfortunately, Tom was not to be our guide. Moreover, we were matched with a third climber whose especially abrasive personality had emerged over the past few days.

Thea and I both felt that this would not do. I went into the Exum office and, price be damned, we hired a private guide, leaving the curmudgeon to his own devices. (We later learned that he'd forced his party to turn around somewhere on the Grand, because he wasn't fit to continue. The waivers signed before the climb acknowledge that the price does not guarantee the summit and that a variety of conditions may force the guide to turn back early. We'd made the right decision to climb without him!)

Our guide was Forest McCarthy, another 30-something Exum superstar who was a bit quieter than Tom. Forest led us on the two-day undertaking. The trailhead to Grand Teton begins at the end of Lupine Meadows, where many of the tenured Exum guides live for the summer in the shadow of the range. The hike is long and strenuous, covering about eight miles up Garnet Canyon. It led past views of Bradley Lake, and the impressive peaks of Nez Perce and Cloudveil Dome on route to the Middle Teton Glacier.

THEA AT MIDDLE TETON GLACIER

Our objective was the Lower Saddle which serves as base camp for the Teton climb. To reach it aspiring climbers get their first taste of the climb by negotiating a slightly precarious fifteen-foot cliff. It can be free climbed for those with experience, but a fixed rope is there to help others along. Once atop this obstacle, the path winds its way steadily up to a plateau beneath the Grand.

After covering this eight-mile stretch over several hours, it is a relief to finally reach the Exum Lower Saddle hut. The hut is an old Quonset type structure with a framework of metal tubes, covered with a heavy plasticized canvas to keep out the elements. It is cabled to the ground and gear is stored outside in a giant metal box which is also lashed to the ground. When the wind blows, inevitably it feels like a gale force wind that could carry the whole structure off the Saddle. The Toilet facilities are as rudimentary as on Gilligan's Island. Between two large boulders is a partially private wooden screen with a toilet seat. Everyone is issued a Reststop 2 - a portable, sealable bag for waste. You hike out whatever you carry in.

There is a lot of activity on the Saddle. Numerous climbing parties play Frisbee, search the Saddle for lost treasure, boulder on rocks, or just hang out waiting for dinner. Everyone eats together in a giant mess as the guides prepare a simple dinner of soup, goulash and fruit. Shortly thereafter, it's lights out so everyone can rest before the early 3:30 AM start. Some guides prefer to sleep outside instead of sharing the Saddle hut with their clients. They have carved out their own personal niches behind or beneath boulders to shield themselves from the relentless winds that roar through the Saddle. Of course it is difficult to sleep despite the tiring hike in, since most first timers to the Grand are anxious for the climb. That night, the wind blew like a hurricane, the covering over the hut flapped relentlessly, and the whole structure shook. My first thought at 3 AM was whether or not the climb would be called due to the high wind. But we were cleared to climb so we geared up and started off for the mountain.

In the early morning darkness, Forest led Thea and me up and over the talus slopes for a half hour beneath the mountain, on a zigzagging path toward the first pitch. The night sky was midnight blue and an endless sea of luminous stars lit our way forward, a good omen for a clear morning. We scrambled on as the path ahead steepened. Occasionally we used handholds on the rock to steady our balance upward. We stopped to rope up, tying our own knots. Forest checked each one to make sure the bowlines were tied correctly, and then we proceeded upward over the first fairly easy, exposed slab.

At this place, the guide decides to ascend either the Exum Ridge or Owen Spalding Route, based on weather and the client's competence on the rock. I had made my mind up months ago that I only wanted to climb the Exum. History means a lot to me, and I had looked forward to climbing the Exum Ridge in part for its historical significance. Directly ahead was a foreboding wall, steep and relentless for a thousand feet up. It was the actual ridge itself. To reach it, we ascended Wall Street, a famous ledge that looks steep from the start, but in reality the guides say you could ride a mountain bike around on it! At each pitch we had to stack the rope, belay, signal each other, and then coil the ropes again before moving on. It was awkward at first. Under pressure, I found myself trying to remember what I'd learned in climbing school so that I could do it right and show competence on the mountain.

The Exum Ridge is a classic climb. Just beyond Wall Street is a seemingly bottomless chasm that must be crossed before taking to the ridge. In July 1931, Glenn Exum reached this place unroped, and, wearing leather football shoes, jumped to the other side. His was a committing and intimidating move. Thea and I belayed safely across without incident. The exposure was ever-present now. The next move was exacting – a stretching reach across to smear your shoe on a small nubbin of a foothold. Weighting the right leg to apply as much friction as possible to the rock protrusion, we had to reach up and to the left to grip an unseen hold. We came to a walled area and used our legs, feet, arms, and hands to apply opposing force on each side for a quick move – known as stemming. The move reminded me of Santa Claus going up and down fireplace chimneys, since the space was that narrow. Many of our belays had to be done in a sitting fashion on ledges with the rope passing behind our back for friction.

The sun's rays appeared over the horizon and cast a beautiful, orangey dawn glow over everything. The rock was solid, the holds plentiful and our confidence built steadily as we rose higher and higher up the mountain. Soon we came to the crux called the Friction Pitch. We ascended one at a time gripping the top edge of this rock with both hands. The balls of our feet smeared flatly on the 60 degree sloping slab about fifty feet long. Below us was an endless void. If the wind is blowing, the natural tendency is to grip the rock close to shield oneself from the feeling of being blown off. But this is bad form and dangerous as it does not provide ideal friction. Looking back from the crux, we saw the quintessential exposed drop, 2,500 feet down to the Middle Teton Glacier below. The view is impressive and it is everyone's idea of what mountain climbing is all about. We took photos as we reached the top of the crux, imagining that someday we'd show them to our kids and grandkids.

Thea negotiates the Wind Slab Friction Pitch

Roger on the crux of the Exum Ridge

We scrambled up rock slopes, holding our ropes coiled for several pitches, and then suddenly we were on the summit. It was a rocky boulder strewn landscape about 30 yards long. The view in all directions was glorious. We were surrounded by mountain ranges, and could see the Wind River, Gros Ventre and even the Lost River Range in Idaho from our perch. Yellowstone National Park, 50 miles away, is also visible, and climbers can even see Old Faithful's hourly bursts. The sun at our backs created a perfect shadow of the pyramidal form of the Grand Teton against the landscape below. We focused our attention on the other great peaks of the range: Mount Owen, Middle Teton, and Teewinot with Jenny and Jackson Lakes below. Seven thousand feet beneath us was the trailhead at Lupine Meadows where our climb began the day before. I reflected in the silence and felt genuinely happy to have achieved this summit on my first attempt. My goal had been the Grand Teton, and I felt satisfied that the ascent had gone smoothly without any weather or other variables to contend with, unlike my experience on the Matterhorn. Thea felt that in-between state of elation and exertion on her first real climb. It always feels a bit surreal until you're down and the accomplishment really sinks in.

The Beaudoins summit the Grand

Grand Teton's shadow

The descent began by scrambling down a few pitches on the Owen Spalding Route to a chimney and then scrambling down again to the start of the rappel point. We were well prepared for the rappel, a 120 foot vertical drop over a steep rocky precipice. The rappel began from a narrow rock platform, like an amusement park ride. I imagined the little man sitting on a stool taking my ticket, and then one by one urging us on. The bottom of the rappel can't be seen from this starting platform. You start by placing your feet shoulder distance apart on the rock and then walking down the wall. You are of course secured by your own belay device and actions. The guide's place a second fail-safe belay on you for extra security, but you're still stepping off that 120 foot cliff and it's impossible not to imagine the possibilities. The first 60 feet seem straightforward, but then the bottom falls away and you hang midair for the duration of the rappel. The trick is to continue your descent without spinning and twisting, easier said than done. It helps if the wind isn't blowing.

The author rappels off the Grand

Forest McCarthy at the summit

I remember little of the rest of the descent after the rappel. I recall seeing switchbacks that lead down through boulder fields. We climbed over the tops of some rock and some we bypassed until eventually the Lower Saddle and Exum hut came into view. From there, it took a while to reach the spartan comfort of the Saddle. After a short rest there, we replenished our water supply and continued trekking down toward our starting point. Prudence dictated a quick descent to avoid the all too common summer thunderstorms. The start of our adventure was eight long miles away and

5,000 vertical feet back down before we reached the Lupine Meadows trailhead. I thought we would never stop walking.

The Whitney Gilman Ridge

Cannon Cliff in Franconia Notch, New Hampshire is another of New England's classic climbs. This immense wall is best known for its former rock feature, symbol of the state: The Old Man of the Mountain, which tumbled down the face in 2003. The imposing Cannon Cliff rises nearly 1,000 feet from the valley below.

A friend, Ben, and I have climbed the North Conway, New Hampshire area for years with our regular guide Conrad Jager. Most of the time we let Conrad decide our objective. But in the summer of 2012, I was eager to try the classic route known as Lakeview. Lakeview is a multi-pitch climb that weaves and traverses its way up the face, topping out at the site of the Old Man. The feature held a strange fascination for me for years, ever since I first saw the recognizable profile of the Old Man's face from far below. Knowing that the climb would end where the face used to be kindled my imagination.

We set out climbing the lower scree field on our way toward Lakeview and got an early start for what we knew would be a long day of climbing. It turned out that there were several parties in front of us, so Conrad wisely decided to avoid Lakeview. Rockfall from above is the main hazard, much like the Matterhorn. It didn't take much convincing to turn our attention to the left skyline, and to a route called the Whitney Gilman Ridge, named for its first summiters.

As we approached the ridge from the boulder field and looked up. We saw a prominent vertical knife-edge that soared a thousand feet to the sky. Conrad told us that this was also a classic route with 6 lengthy pitches to the top. The notorious crux is called the Pipe Pitch, named for the old broken pipe used as a belay on the first ascent that still juts out from the rock today.

WHITNEY GILMAN RIDGE, CANNON CLIFF

We arrived at the base and met a party of three whom we briefly chatted with before we watched them tackle the first pitch. When it was time to move, Conrad set the lead upward and started to place protection. Ben followed upon command as I waited for my turn as third on the rope. Going last means you remove each piece of protection as you ascend and secure it to your harness or a sling around your upper body. We gained altitude quickly and the exposure below and to the side was immediately obvious. We were climbing just to the left of the Black Dike, an infamous ice climb route in the winter. This section of the cliff looks like a massive, ominous elevator shaft and is known for perilous, thin ledges. Having it in view while ascending the Whitney Gilman was especially foreboding.

The pitches were satisfying to climb at first, but became increasingly difficult as the hours passed. The wind picked up, adding to the challenge and it became nearly impossible to hear Conrad's commands or communicate with him. At about this time we reached the crux – the well-known Pipe Pitch – which was the most challenging part of the climb. My mind started to wander and I wondered how Conrad would be able to assist from high above if Ben or I were stuck and unable to ascend the wall. Somehow Ben was able to overcome the difficulties and exposure. As I attempted the obvious line, it would not go, and I struggled. There was an awkward overhang above and to the right, so clinging to the rock, I fought to find the holds. My body was contorted out in space and I hesitantly looked down at least 700 feet at the Black Dike. The wind howled around me.

Negotiating the second pitch on Cannon Cliff

Another party approached from below and quickly caught up to me. I exchanged pleasantries with the 20-something lead climber who complimented me saying, "I never seen any 50 year old up here before." My pride swelled. His words provided just the confidence boost I needed to overcome the Pipe Pitch, though the sequence of moves I used to master the overhanging crux remains a blur.

Black Dike, Cannon Cliff

The last two pitches were straightforward, yet challenging as we weaved our way to top out. Fifty yards from the top, trees began to appear, growing out of the rocks and the vertical cliff morphed into forest. The trees below were beginning to turn red and gold. Fall was in the air. Far below, vehicles slowly winding their way along the Kancamagus Highway looked like matchbox cars. As we emerged from the immense, unrelenting exposure onto a flat narrow trail leading through the woods, it felt like we'd reached Middle-earth in J.R.R. Tolkien's trilogy. We followed the woodland trail into the forest, which quickly swallowed the view. The path wound its way left, running parallel to the top of the cliff before sloping down, pointing us back toward the base of the climb. We made the hike down in an hour, returning to reality to join the regular mortals enjoying Franconia Notch. We looked up at the Whitney Gilman Ridge one last time for good measure before heading back to North Conway for a pizza and well-earned glass of red wine.

Katahdin

I am a member of the Mahoosuc Mountain Search and Rescue Team in Maine. We volunteers assist the Maine Warden's Service and bring aid to lost or injured hikers or climbers. Sometimes we carry them out of deep woods or coordinate helicopter evacuations. Occasionally we're called in to assist police units for body searches or recoveries. In addition to our regular duties in our home range the Mahoosucs, on several summer weekends we assist park rangers in Baxter State Park. The park is the home of Katahdin, New England's second tallest peak and the final destination for north bound "through hikers" on the famed Appalachian Trail (AT). The park is so vast and there is such a surge in hiking and visitor traffic during the summer months, that the regular park ranger staff frequently needs our assistance. These are committing weekends, as the drive to the park is five hours each way and as most of the popular hikes cover many miles of difficult terrain.

As a veteran climber of Mount Washington, numerous people have asked if I'd summited Katahdin. I had heard of the infamous Knife Edge many times, but the opportunity to summit Katahdin did not present itself until I joined Mahoosuc. My first chance at the peak happened in the summer of 2011 when I was training for my second Matterhorn attempt. One weekend I joined Jim, one of my climbing partners for the Swiss trip, and we manned the Search & Rescue cabin at Togue Pond in Baxter State Park. Togue is miles by car from the Roaring Brook Trailhead, and miles more on foot up to the base of Katahdin. So an early morning start is essential to summit and return back the same day.

As often happens in the mountains, heavy rain and fog all weekend kept us from attempting the Knife Edge or any other route up Katahdin. We did some lesser hikes in the area, but really got a workout when we responded to a rescue call to carry out a 250-pound Boy Scout leader who had broken his ankle in the woods. Fortunately, he was only about a mile from the trailhead when we joined the first responders who had already loaded him onto a collapsible litter. These carryouts can take 12 hours or more depending on the distance from safety and the ruggedness of terrain. Generally fifteen or more volunteer hands are needed to share the load and take turns relieving one another from the strenuous dead weight of the victim. The Scout leader was in pain which was exacerbated by the bumpy carryout. It poured on us as if we were in the Vietnam jungle, and the going was rough as we carried the heavy victim over boulders, around trees, and through the mud on the narrow trail to the waiting ambulance.

The following year, Mahoosuc Search & Rescue stayed at Chimney Pond cabin in close proximity of the peak. Chimney Pond lies at the base of Katahdin's immense glacial cirque, and as with the Riffelsee and Matterhorn in Switzerland, it reflects a beautiful image of the mountain in its glassy water. To reach Chimney, you hike the four-mile Roaring Brook Trail through dense forest up to the tree line. This is one of the more beautiful hikes in New England, teasing with glorious views of Katahdin and its satellite peaks along the way.

KATAHDIN CIRQUE, MAINE

Our first training day found us bushwhacking up into the cirque. We were following some climbers who appeared to be taking a dangerous route up the lower slabs on the flank of the mountain, heading toward a popular climbing route called the Armadillo. As soon as we got within striking distance, one of the climbers kicked down some loose rock that quickly escalated into a cascade of falling stones, nearly striking us. We had to take immediate cover and make ourselves as small as possible, hunkering down against the wall or behind larger rocks to avoid disaster. The climbers made it safely up the Armadillo and no further instances were reported by the lead ranger who vigilantly monitors all the major routes via binoculars from his base at Chimney Pond.

Much to my disappointment, none of the veteran Search & Rescue guys felt like climbing Katahdin the following day. As with Mount Washington in New Hampshire, Katahdin is a serious summit not to be undertaken without proper preparation. I considered myself capable of going solo. (Remember my first trek to touch the Matterhorn?) But then I thought better of the idea. I was older now and an old heel injury was giving me trouble. I began to doubt myself, and I had visions of the rescuer needing a rescue: not an attractive thought. As an alternative, Bob Baribeau, one of the leaders of the Mahoosuc Mountain Search and Rescue Team and a man who had accomplished many of the first ascents on Katahdin's difficult ice routes, led us on a hike of the Hamlin Ridge to Hamlin Peak. Named for Hannibal Hamlin, the 15th Vice President of the U.S. who served under Abraham Lincoln, the route was long and strenuous. The hike required some rock scrambling and led in the direction of Katahdin's summit, but we did not top out there and it was not as intense as the infamous Knife Edge. We spent our downtime on this glorious, sunny weekend looking up with binoculars at Katahdin's most challenging routes to wait for rescue calls that never came.

Third Time's the Charm

On my third visit to Baxter in the summer of 2013, I stayed with members of my team at the Togue Pond shelter. We went our separate route on Saturday morning but Jerry and Nicole, two new members, were game to attempt the summit with me. After an early start from Roaring Brook, we made decent time to Chimney Pond and signed in at the Ranger Station. I had no doubt about which route to take, and I assertively suggested we pursue the most challenging, heading for Katahdin's Baxter Peak. The steepest way up the mountain is via the exposed Cathedral Trail which quickly gets your heart pumping once you pass the tree line. Cathedral has three prominent rock precipices that lead to the summit as you ascend higher. Feeling jubilant about finally being on route to the top of Katahdin, I set a fast pace at the start. Soon Nicole experienced some difficulty. I looked back and saw Jerry helping her negotiate some steep boulders. Unbeknownst to me, Nicole had a fear of heights and was a bit freaked by the exposure down the cirque. Nonetheless, we all continued upward.

Cathedral Trail, with our destination Baxter Peak on the left

The wind had been blowing almost from the start. At one point on Cathedral Trail, Jerry's hat blew off and we watched it sail like a kite down into the cirque. The wind was raging by the time we topped out, intensified by the flat plateau that surrounds Baxter Peak. A wooden sign on the summit marks the northern terminus of the Appalachian Trail. A long queue of through-hikers jockeyed to take photos by the sign, commemorating the completion of their 2,100-mile journey.

At the Summit of Mount Katahdin

Jerry, Nicole, and I sat and had lunch on jagged rocks just below the summit out of the wind. I thought after the exposure on Cathedral that Nicole would choose to go down the easier Saddle Route back to

Chimney. But to her credit I was amazed that she wanted to continue on our intended route. There is no greater challenge, nor more committing hike to be found anywhere in the East than the Knife Edge of Katahdin – especially with the wind gusting around us.

Mount Katahdin's Infamous Knife Edge

I'd heard plenty of descriptions of this route, but none did the trek justice. Almost immediately, we found ourselves scrambling up, over, and around jagged rock outcroppings that, at their widest, were about four feet and with sheer vertical drops of 1,000 feet on either side. Our windproof nylon jackets acted like sails, and more than once I thought we'd be blown off our feet. I pictured Jerry's hat, gently drifting down into the depths of the cirque, knowing that if one of us were to fall, the trajectory would be more gruesome. The heavy wind slowed our pace and we inched our way for almost two hours, headed toward Pamola Peak at the other end of the Knife's Edge. Just before stepping off the last of the difficult sections, we came to the chimney. We almost needed a rope to descend the steep cliff drop, but with focus we were able to spider down feet first, searching carefully for minuscule holds as we went.

We were surprised to see a father with an infant in a backpack and another small child in tow several miles from the trailhead. None of them were dressed for weather. It was late in the day and they did not seem to have food or water. With our search & rescue experience, this seemed to be an imprudent accident waiting to happen, but we continued down after the father assured us he was not going much farther up the trail towards Knife's Edge. After the long day we'd logged, the trek from Pamola back to Roaring Brook was relentless and seemed never ending. Back at the cabin, we reveled in our Katahdin memories with the team over a hearty dinner. The following day we left Baxter State Park, another rescue-free weekend safely completed.

8

A SIXTY FOOT FALL

In 2011, I felt that old pull. Again Matterhorn was the magnet drawing me in. It had been ten years since I last visited Zermatt and nine since I climbed a mountain. If I did make a second climb, my return would be fueled by both hubris and a desire to repeat the past. For the Matterhorn had shaped my life and been my proudest accomplishment. Still I needed to test myself. Was I was worthy of its challenge one more time?

Before committing to a second attempt, I felt compelled to think about what had happened to me two years before. I thought about how lucky I was even to be alive, let alone to think of tackling the mountain again. It had only been two years since I'd nearly lost my life in a terrible fall. I'd started training with the thought of making a second climb. By all accounts, after the fall, I shouldn't be alive today.

A Fine Line

The year was 2009 and the day was glorious – one of those sunny, beautiful, bluebird September days. I simply had to be outside. Thea had run 20 miles that morning and I had driven her and her running partner to the start of their run. Driving through Grafton Notch in Maine on my way home, I had that old familiar urge to get out and climb. None of my usual climbing partners were available, so I stopped by a new friend's house and asked if he wanted to learn. Steve was adventurous and intrigued by new challenges, and over the years I had taught half a dozen newbies the basics of climbing, belaying, and rappelling.

We went to Tumbledown, the local crag, and spent the next four hours trying various routes. Steve had good basic climbing skills and seemed to quickly pick up the practice of belaying. Toward mid-afternoon, Steve said he was tired, but asked if I would like one more climb before heading home. Call it hubris, a false sense of security, or just not knowing when to quit, but it was one of those days when I had not had enough. We agreed to one final climb.

Tumbledown, the site of my accident

Standard practice calls for climbers to check each other's knots, harness and gear before every climb. The harness waist and leg belts need be doubled back. The figure eight knot attached to the climber must be tied correctly and then properly tied in to his harness. Most importantly, the belayer's carabiner and belay device must be attached to the belay loop on his harness with the carabiner gate screwed tight and locked down. This belay loop is fail-tested and typically designed to withstand five thousand pounds of force before it fails. We had performed these checks conscientiously all afternoon, but failed to do so for this last climb. Without checking Steve's gear, I got into position to make the last climb of the day.

Steve gave the signal "belay on." I responded back, "climbing," and up I went. The first 25 feet of our final cliff was a steeply slanting slab interspersed with slippery moss that required delicate moves on small holds. I focused on moving quickly and methodically to the next hold before the first crux was reached. At this point the slope became nearly vertical, but the holds were good and the climbing was straightforward until I reached the gear. As I reached the top of our top-rope setup, my phone rang. I pulled it out of my pocket and seeing Thea's name on the caller ID, I decided to wait to return her call once I was back on the firm ground. I called down to tell Steve that I was ready to rappel and then I leaned back in my harness with both feet against the vertical wall. I anticipated the relaxed, vertical walk down the wall that characterizes a normal belay, a descent under the complete control of the belayer.

Instantly, I began falling far too quickly. I knew I was out of control. Something was terribly wrong and I could not stop myself. I was dropping all the way to the bottom, the equivalent of falling off a six-story building. Time seemed to move forward and stand still simultaneously. I was tumbling through the air yet I had time to think even as I fell from the cliff face. I remember hitting my head hard as I tumbled backwards. Then the lights went out. I saw bright flashing lights as if the flashbulbs of 100 cameras went off in my face. To say the moment was surreal is an understatement. I was lucid enough to wonder if I had died. Was this what it is like to come out on the other side?

Miraculously, I hit the ground landing on my feet, but the momentum from the fall had me ragdolling for another 30 yards or so. Suddenly my forward motion was violently arrested. Gear had broken free from Steve's harness and had lodged in the carabiners that attached our rope at the top of the cliff face. This put an end to my out-of-control tumble as I was attached to the other end of this system. The accident was caused by Steve inadvertently clipping the belay device and carabiner into a weak gear loop on the side of his harness instead of the fail-safe belay loop directly in front of him. As soon as I weighted the rope from above when I began my rappel, the gear loop immediately failed and ripped from the harness releasing me and the gear from the belay.

I opened my eyes and found myself lying flat on my back between two jagged rocks on either side of my body. They were close enough that I could have lifted both arms and rested them on these rocks. But miraculously I hadn't hit them.

Steve ran to me and in a panic, asked, "What do we do?" I told him to call 911. But after phoning in the emergency, he handed me the phone. He'd never been to Tumbledown and couldn't tell the operator our location. I was dazed but lucid enough to direct the EMTs to our location. Then Steve called Thea, who didn't recognize his phone number and didn't answer. Thankfully Steve's wife Janet reached Thea, but Janet couldn't provide Thea any information about the severity of my injury.

Steve told me that I banged my head hard on the rock cliff during my first somersault, and that I'd somersaulted once or twice more before hitting the ground. I wasn't wearing a helmet, since typically they are only worn when there is danger of falling rock from above.

I lay motionless on the ground, knowing that at a minimum, I had a broken foot. I could feel pain and knew from prior experience that I had broken bones. But in moments like this the pain is actually muted by the intensity of the trauma. I was aware of a peculiar feeling and I touched the back of my head. It was soaked in blood. My first thought was brain trauma and I worried that although the impact hadn't killed me, I could still lapse into a coma and die. I kept my hand on my head and wondered if my brains were exposed. I was too scared to ask Steve.

My friend Chris Hayward, a leader of the Mahoosuc Mountain Search and Rescue Team, came into my field of vision. Chris was in first responder mode, took my vital signs, and reported that my pulse was steady. I likely had a concussion and was probably in shock, but I was glad to see him. I remember saying, "Good to see you, Chris."

The ambulance arrived soon afterwards and luckily for the EMTs, I was close to the road and didn't need a long, technical carryout. I was loaded on a backboard, transferred to a gurney, and carried into the ambulance. Thea had arrived to join me for the ride to the hospital. She'd been told only that I'd broken my ankle and was unaware of the full extent of my injuries. In the ambulance, I was given oxygen and one of the EMTs continually monitored my vital signs. The bumpy 40-minute ride to the hospital felt like an eternity. Thea and I shared a look of concern when halfway there, the ambulance stopped to pick up an expert for my case.

I spent the next six hours in the ER. I was given every CT scan known to man: head, internal organs, and beyond. Every medical person who came in contact with me was amazed at the limited extent of my injuries considering the height I fell from. Amazingly, the scans showed nothing alarming. I was diagnosed with only a pulverized calcaneus (heel). It was shattered into 13 pieces. I needed ten stitches in the back of my head, but my brains were not sticking out, nor did I have any head trauma.

Steve and Janet arrived and brought me breakfast cereal which I devoured. We spent a few hours with nurses who extracted bits of gravel and leaves from my neck and back. Despite my injuries, they commented on my high tolerance for pain, lack of complaints, and easy nature. My doctors scheduled a heel operation for later that week. I was finally released and sent home on crutches.

Dr. Dirk Asherman, my orthopedic surgeon, was young, confident, and skilled. Reattaching the 13 pieces of my heel required numerous plates, pins, and screws. Dr. Asherman said my heel looked like it had been reduced to dust. I was amazed at Dr. Asherman's work and my foot healed over time. Ski season was rapidly approaching and there was even a glimmer of hope that I would be back on the slopes by mid-January. That thought motivated me during physical therapy sessions. I'd had surgeries before and was always eager to do the work required to regain my strength and range of motion.

On the Long Road to Recovery

After months of rehab, my ankle stubbornly remained swollen and the size of a grapefruit. I couldn't get my ski boot on but I was impatient to get outdoors and play in the snow. My first outing of the season was in snowshoes. I figured that would be a low-impact way to return to physical activity. I would work my way back to skiing and climbing. I overexerted myself snowshoeing and exacerbated my condition by icing my foot without a layer of protection. I got frostbite!

Several weeks after my snowshoeing incident, it was time to try skiing. I strapped on skis and completed half a run, but my swollen foot was in intense pain. It felt like I'd need the Jaws of Life to get my ski boot off. I'm not sure how I even got it on with the swelling in my ankle. Undeterred, a week later I figured that if I couldn't ski, maybe I could ice climb. My local ice cliff is the Amphitheatre which has a 20-minute hike-in to get to the wall. I limped in and roped up, climbing high on several of the routes. I was not freaked out at all by the exposure and did not experience any stress afterwards. I took that as an encouraging sign.

By mid-summer, nearly a year after my fall, there had been virtually no reduction in the swelling in my foot. I saw another surgeon for a second opinion. I tested negative for infections and the surgeon was stumped. I went back to Dr. Asherman and he suggested that maybe I was having a negative reaction to all the hardware in my foot. We decided to go back in and remove it all and scheduled surgery. I went back under the knife.

Immediately following the second surgery, I felt a dramatic change. My body literally rejoiced and the swelling began to subside. I was optimistic that things would soon be back to normal, but as with any surgery, I now had to worry about the possibility of infection. Sure enough, bacteria found its way down one of the holes in my bone left by the hardware, and my foot swelled up again.

I was referred to a bone infection specialist in Maine for treatment, who recommended hooking me up to an IV for six weeks to treat me with continuous antibiotics. Concerned about the limits this would impose on physical activity, sleep, and the other annoyances, I asked if there were any alternatives. My other option was an oral antibiotic, but the drawback was that you had to avoid direct sunlight while taking the medication; otherwise your skin burns and feels like you poured acid on it. Although I was scheduled to travel to the Bahamas for a scuba trip and would be on the dive boat every day for a week, I chose the second option. Luckily I avoided the acid torture, but I worried about it every day in the tropical sun.

Gradually I recovered. I rededicated myself to intense physical therapy and conditioning, with the dream of a second Matterhorn climb as a constant inspiration. My first successful summit in 1998 had been a surreal, almost out of body experience and I found myself craving a return. I had an endless fascination with this mountain and nothing could keep me from it. I wanted to validate my first climb, and relive the experience. I also began re-experiencing the surreal animated dreams I'd had of climbing the mountain which I occasionally still have to this day.

The harder the therapy exercises, the more motivated I felt. I did countless repetitions of range of motion exercises on my damaged foot. I'd wake up with stiffness in my ankle joint and would limp down the stairs every morning. If I touched my foot along the lengthy incision, I felt intense nerve tingling and tenderness. I worked hard to strengthen myself, push my limits, and adapt with the nerve tingling as a new standard of normalcy. The nerve tingling lingers even now, years later, although it has lessened with time. I often replay my accident in my mind - almost like a statistical game. If I were to fall off that cliff ten more times, each time

I would almost certainly die or be paralyzed. Remarkably, I had the joy of climbing again.

9

ONCE MORE TO THE TOP

After climbing Wyoming's Grand Teton in 2002, my life changed. I got married, built a house, and for a while my priorities shifted. I continued to rock climb near my home, but the inner force to climb major peaks seemed to have all but disappeared.

It would return. In 2011 a friend, Ben, instigated my return to the Matterhorn. Ben was an adventurous, non-climber who'd been inspired by my summit photographs. I introduced him to rock climbing and each summer for years we hired a guide to lead us up Cathedral Ledge and to other crags in the White Mountains of New Hampshire. Then Ben made the trip to Zermatt where he too was awestruck when he saw the great mountain from a distance. He suggested we make a climb happen. Ben's half-brother Jim was also intrigued. Of course I needed precious little convincing.

I approached a second Matterhorn climb as a personal challenge. After all, I enjoyed being the voice of experience and introducing others to my passion. However the prospect of another climb – even with successful summits already under my belt – brought back the full range of all of my familiar feelings: intimidation, fear, excitement, and awe. The Matterhorn holds an undeniable power over me, and I am certain that if another attempt were on my horizon even today, I'd feel the same way. But for Ben and Jim, ignorance was bliss. They weren't especially anxious. They had done little research and for the most part were completely unfamiliar with the challenges of climbing the Matterhorn.

Another aspiring climber, Don, a friend of Ben's from New York City, joined our party as well. Don had actually been in on the plan since the beginning, but had his own ideas about the climb. Instead of following my advice and hiring a seasoned Zermatt Swiss guide, Don found his own guide from America who happened to have a home in Crested Butte, Colorado. While the rest of us postponed the trip originally planned for 2010 due to my injury, Don ventured solo to the Matterhorn. He was unsuccessful in his first summit attempt and planned to return with us to try again in 2011.

Preparing for Victory

I mapped out a rigorous training plan that included an ascent of Cathedral Ledge, numerous hikes of Mount Washington and other strenuous climbs that included a few rappels. Weekend after weekend over the summer of 2011 we set to work getting fit and preparing to take on the Matterhorn…or so I thought. Jim and I were the only two who took our training seriously. Ben, freshly divorced, spent more time dating than training. We would find out later exactly what Ben's training plan had been. Don was the classic "Type-A" personality and prepared intensely for the Matterhorn. He had one prior attempt under his belt and knew what to expect.

Tumbledown, the site of my near-fatal fall, remained my most frequent climbing area. Tumbledown's cliffs have a series of levels. The upper tier, one of my favorite climbs, has a long, committing rappel. I took Jim there one weekend to get him comfortable with long rappels. We were only a few months out from our trip and I still had a serious limp which concerned me. Nevertheless, I ascended the cliff to set the gear, rappelled down numerous times and then climbed up to retrieve the gear.

The following week we traveled to hike Mount Blue in Maine. The trail to the summit is steep, rocky, and strenuous and includes an interesting scramble inside a dark chimney in the rock that surrounds as though you are climbing up into a cave. At its steepest part, a few iron ladder rungs have been installed to assist hikers up and out of the hole. I had no problems on the ascent, but half way down, my limp became debilitating and I had to rely on a trekking pole as a crutch. Even when Jim and I reached the trailhead, we still had to walk a mile or so back to the car. I could not carry on and had to wait on the side of the road while Jim went for the car and picked me up. Although I've always been a confident climber, I was beginning to doubt that my foot would recover sufficient strength for the demands of the Matterhorn.

Huntington Ravine is the most difficult route up Mount Washington. The starting point is Pinkham Notch Base Camp, and the hiking is straightforward if not monotonous for the first two miles. Once you hike up into the base of the ravine, the route quickly turns into an engaging rock scramble up steep, slippery slabs. The grade is rated 5.6, just on the verge of requiring ropes. It is incredibly dangerous when wet. The rangers strongly advise against down climbing Huntington Ravine, and they suggest avoiding it entirely following recent rainfall.

One Saturday, Jim and I set off for Huntington. We reached the base of the slabs in two hours and as soon as we did, it started to rain. We turned around and down we went. Shoulder-high scrub brush lined the trail for much of the hike, and though finding the route on the ascent is relatively easy, Jim and I got lost coming down. Our only option was to bushwhack in search of the path of least resistance.

Several weeks later we returned to Huntington to complete our ascent of the ravine. I had no trouble on the way up, but once again my left foot stiffened and sent sharp pains up my leg forcing me to limp back down the four plus miles to Pinkham Notch. At that point it was only two months until our planned departure for Switzerland. I was very concerned because Huntington is similar to the trek to the base of the Matterhorn and as demanding. I wondered if my pain would return when it would really be a problem on the Matterhorn.

Destination: Zermatt

On the day I flew from Portland, Maine to Switzerland, Jim and I had lunch at a favorite Mexican restaurant, sharing margaritas to toast the trip. I had booked an earlier flight than my climbing partners and looked forward to two days by myself in Zermatt. Perhaps because I grew up as an only child, I like some solitary time when I can be alone with my thoughts. I felt I had trained hard, and I had lined up three Zermatt guides. All I needed now was for the weather to cooperate.

My flight was uneventful and unlike all previous trips, I flew for the first time into Geneva, the closest major airport to Zermatt. I boarded the train and soon after pulling out of the station, delighted in the scenery: Lake Geneva's long shorelines, the lowland hills and vineyards along the countryside, the countless villages, train stops and the distant peaks. For me these experiences have always seemed more like a fantasy than reality. Two short hours later, I arrived in the town of Visp. Before transferring to the familiar red Glacier Express train, I picked up a simple European lunch from a small market in the center of town: a French baguette, some cheese and bottle of local red wine. I sat on the platform to wait my train, enjoying my meal and the sights and sounds of Europe.

Slightly buzzed from the wine, I sat contentedly in my seat and surveyed the familiar scene of glacial waterfalls cascading down the steep narrow gorge of the Visp Valley. The train chugged past the quaint village stops that I had always admired from out a window yet had never ventured to visit. First came Stalden, followed by St. Niklaus and then Randa. I was excited about this trip and my mind wandered back to my first Glacier Express ride some 23 years earlier. I smiled at the memory of switching from window seat to window seat in search of the best view, completely enamored by this little slice of the world.

As always I was impatient to reach Zermatt, and today was no exception. The dark final tunnel between Tasch and Zermatt heightened my anticipation until finally the Glacier Express pulled into the station. I got off the train, walked through the bustling town square, and headed south up the Bahnhofstrasse to the Hotel Antika where I'd spend the night.

My basement annex room was tiny, but the bed and down comforter were cozy and I had a small private bath. I settled in quickly and then retraced my old footsteps through Zermatt taking photos and visiting familiar haunts. I was disappointed to find the North Wall Bar closed for the summer. It had been turned into a ski tuning room for one of the national ski teams that was training on the glacier. Instead I wandered into a place just off the Bahnhof Hotel terrace, drawn by the promise of an arugula salad with shaved Parmesan. That sounded just right. I sat outside on the patio, drank a beer and people watched. The sunset cast an orangey-pink alpenglow over the Alps as dusk poured over the surrounding peaks. The Matterhorn rested like the crown jewel in the alpine setting.

The next morning I awoke early, my mind racing with the thrill of the impending climb. I headed out to the street and snapped photo after photo of the dawn breaking. I was awestruck by the way the light shifted over the Matterhorn's majestic form, making each shot uniquely different. The optical illusion was particularly convincing from my vantage point, and I found myself wondering how on earth the Matterhorn was climbable, much as Whymper and his companions must have wondered nearly 150 years earlier.

Breakfast at the Antika was glorious. The traditional dining room was outfitted with heavy wooden tables and chairs with heart shaped cutouts in the seatbacks. It didn't hurt that I was ravenous, but the fresh crusty bread and jams, creamy Swiss yogurts, muesli and tea were immensely satisfying. After breakfast, I checked out of the Antika and into the more luxurious apartment I had rented for Ben, Jim and myself for the duration of our stay. As usual, Don had other plans and was staying solo in a nearby hotel. Our apartment, directly across the lane from the North Wall Bar, was surprisingly affordable, modern and comfortable with a great terrace view of the Matterhorn.

I spent the day in Zermatt, acclimating and anticipating the arrival of my friends. I was standing outside a sports shop on one of the quiet side streets when a mountain biker zoomed past and then came to a quick stop. "Roger!" the biker exclaimed. I could hardly believe it. Eleven years after our first meeting, Helmut Lerjen recognized me instantly. We went to a nearby restaurant and caught up over a drink. Helmut was to be my guide for the upcoming climb, and we felt a kinship as we discussed our training hikes and plans for the Matterhorn. Helmut felt the weather would change for the worse in the next few days and suggested that we climb sooner rather than later. We didn't have time to wait out bad weather, and we needed to get in several hikes at altitude before our major ascent.

While I waited for Jim, Ben and Don to arrive, I stepped into a sport shop and bought a new Mammut pack for the Matterhorn. Mammut is a prestigious, iconic Swiss brand of outdoor gear and I was pleased with my purchase.

After shopping, once again the Matterhorn cemetery beckoned and I found myself walking the headstones in morbid curiosity. The epitaphs always humbled me. I reflected on the people who died and remembered the accidents I'd witnessed with my own eyes. Standing amidst the mountain-shaped tombstones, it's impossible to avoid knowing that nature always wins and that even the most skilled climbers can't prevent the inevitable. Like those lost climbers, I too am fueled by passion, adventure, and adrenaline, the combination that led to my own near-death accident. It was a crux I had overcome. This realization, tempered with a visit to the mountainside chapel for prayer before the climb, set me straight again and I left the cemetery feeling at peace.

A short time later I greeted the Glacier Express as it pulled into the station carrying Ben, Jim and Don. I was excited to see them and get brought up to date on the walk up Bahnhofstrasse on route to our apartment. True to form, Ben announced that he was hungry and bought a Wurst with mustard and crunchy bread from a sidewalk vendor outside the local butchery.

The three of us settled into our apartment, eventually making our way to the outdoor terrace to take in the Matterhorn and discuss the morning's training plan. Our guides joined us that evening and over wine, discussed preparations for our climb. They said that the mountain was climbable, but that the snowline was lower than the Solvayhutte and that we would need our crampons earlier than usual. By comparison, in 1998 we had put our crampons on at the start of the shoulder, one pitch above the Solvayhutte and two pitches further than we would need them now. Putting them on sooner would slow our progress and make the climbing more challenging since crampons on rock are more awkward than mountaineering boots and require a more focused technique.

Besides my guide Helmut, Kurt Lauber (guide, rescuer and hutkeeper) had arranged for Jim's guide, Johann Williner and Ben's guide Ricki Lehner. Johann looked like a rock star or a Cherokee Indian, with long dark hair and demeanor of bravado. Ben's guide, Ricki Lehner, was famous for a record-breaking rescue in 2010 on Annapurna, a dangerous 8,000 meter peak in the Himalayas. Three Spanish climbers had been stranded in bad weather for 36 hours until they were evacuated from the mountain at 6,900 meters on a long line from a helicopter. Ricki, dangling from the chopper at the end of the line, lifted the stranded climbers one by one to safety. This was the highest long line rescue in history and was especially dangerous because a helicopter's rotor blades lose lift in the high altitude and thin air of the Himalayas. Despite Ricki's incredible heroics, he never mentioned it and we only learned about it from others after our Matterhorn climb.

Our guides advised that considering the weather, we'd have only one day to train before trekking up to the Hornlihutte where our Matterhorn climb would begin. I decided that our destination for the training climb should be the Mettelhorn, a lofty 3,406 meter peak just below the icy white shroud of the Weisshorn: the perfect altitude for acclimatization with a total altitude gain of 1,800 feet. The hike takes the better part of a day. It winds up the steep Trift Valley, then branches right over rocky glacial moraines on route to the Mettelhorn glacier. The glacier itself is about two hundred yards long and is considered safe to cross since it doesn't have hidden crevasses. The Mettelhorn peak sits just beyond the far edge of the glacier and requires a scramble up a narrow trail over loose scree and ledge to reach the highest point. The view from the top is spectacular in good weather and offers climbers a panorama of all 32 of Zermatt's 4,000 meter peaks.

The Second Summit

We got an early start just after dawn and I was full of energy. I had been to the Mettelhorn solo many times before and was excited to lead my friends on this intense challenge. Once past the Trift Hotel and civilization, the rest of the climb is above tree line and you are exposed. Getting caught in fog or in an electrical storm is a common hazard, but many rock tower cairns mark the path. Hours later when we reached the glacier, it was strange to see several people putting on crampons. I had always crossed the glacier wearing only my boots. But on closer inspection, I realized the glacier was no longer there. In its place there was only a downward slope of jagged rock covered with thin ice. Global warming clearly affected the once imposing glacier, and it was virtually gone.

The Mettelhorn peak, left. Receding glacier in the foreground: 2011

We were dangerously unprepared and proceeded slowly across the former glacier without crampons. After about thirty yards, it became clear how unsafe the path was. Each of us slipped on the thin ice and struggled to maintain our footing. It would have been all too easy to fall and rocket downward, bouncing over sharp, jagged rocks with no means of arrest. I turned everyone back, explaining the dangers of our situation. Ben resisted and stubbornly continued for a few more minutes until he realized it was fruitless. Gingerly we repeated our steps until we were safely back on the moraine. There would be no further climbing for us that day.

We sat on the rocks and had lunch, taking in the marvelous scene before us: The Monte Rosa massif with its satellite peaks; Pollux and Castor–the twins; Breithorn, Kleine Matterhorn and the Matterhorn itself; Dent Blanche and Obergabelhorn. They seemed close enough to touch. After following the swift Triftbach Falls down the valley back to Zermatt, we soaked our tired muscles in the whirlpools at the Hotel Eden and reviewed the day. So much for our first training exercise: we hadn't reached the required height, and now we would have to climb without spending adequate time at altitude.

HAVING LUNCH ON THE EDGE OF THE METTELHORN GLACIER WITH BEN; 2011

The next day, Ben, Jim and I set out before noon for the Hornlihutte. Don was training with his own guide who had scheduled their climb a few days later despite the weather info we had received from our local guides. In the days of first ascents, climbers trekked up into the mountains directly from the village without the luxury of modern ski lifts. We cut what would have been a five-hour hike from Zermatt to the Hornlihutte in half by taking the gondola to Schwartzsee. It was still a laborious two and a half hour undertaking, made brighter by the fine summer sun. I once counted 92 zigzags in the trail leading up to the Hornlihutte. The approach is relentless but worth the effort for the amazing view of the Matterhorn at the end. The trail stops at the edge of the Hornlihutte's stone terrace, where guides, Matterhorn aspirants and tourists stand shoulder to shoulder, enjoying the view of the great peak looming above.

As always, we were greeted at the Hornlihutte by a raucous crowd seated at heavy wooden tables drinking beer in the shadow of the Matterhorn. When we arrived, Johann and Ricki were holding court with the other guides, but Helmut was nowhere to be seen. The late afternoon sun dropped below the glacier and with it, the temperature dropped too. It was time to go in for dinner although Helmut had still not arrived. As we ate our meal, we heard the sound of an approaching Air Zermatt chopper getting louder and louder until it landed on the roof. Kurt Lauber, keeper of the Hornlihutte, told me that Helmut who had just arrived in the chopper was taking off for a rescue on the Dent Blanche. Two Spanish climbers had sent out a distress signal from the mountain, but their exact position was unknown. I wondered how this would affect my climb in the early morning and if I would have a replacement guide.

The Hornlihutte was unchanged from when I was there for my first summit in 1998. The walls were moldy, weeping from moisture. The bathroom was still a lofty perch outside the hut where waste fell hundreds of feet to the glacier below. Rows of bunks were sardined in tight formation, offering climbers little personal space. At least thirty people share a room, and if the anxiety about the coming day doesn't keep you awake, the snores from the crowded room certainly will.

Climbers at the Hornlihutte share a common goal, brought together for the same reason. But the pre-climb rituals vary from climber to climber. Mine was to lie awake and think about the day ahead imagining the challenges I would face. I didn't know if Helmut would still climb after the rescue. As always, I was intimidated and respectful of the unknown. Sleep came in fitful spurts. Any dreams I had were fueled by adrenaline and anxiety. I awoke in the middle of the night to the sound of rotor blades. It was Helmut returning from the rescue. I fell back asleep for what seemed like minutes. The next thing I knew it was 3:15 AM.

3:15 AM came quickly. Ben, Jim and I in a drowsy state dressed, assembled our gear, and went downstairs for breakfast where we were met by our guides including Helmut. I was astonished and moved beyond belief as Helmut exemplified the true definition of hero… almost super-human. Unable to locate the stricken climbers shielded in dense fog, he was lowered on to the face of the mountain and spent most of the night climbing perilous terrain solo in the dark searching for them. Once found, Helmut radioed his position to Air Zermatt, then one by one attached the climbers to the chopper's long-line before they could be flown, each individually, to safety. This procedure took hours before Helmut himself was picked up and delivered back to the Hornlihutte, without time to sleep before our climb.

The dining room before a climb has a schoolboy feel. Everyone jockeys for a place at a table close to the door. Some guides attempt to be the first outside since it is safest to be among the first climbers on the mountain. There's less chance that climbers will kick loose rocks down from above.

Being among the first out was my strategy when Richard and I climbed in 1998, and it was unchanged with Helmut now. The crusty bread, jam and tea we consumed was the calm before the storm. I took my tea with lots of sugar for an energy boost and savored this last luxury before our adventure.

Helmut and I peeled off from Jim, Ben and their guides, roped up, and headed out the door into the cold black night. Visibility was limited to what we could see in the narrow beam of our headlamps. The crisp snow crunched beneath our boots, and I followed Helmut's footsteps as we headed toward the first cliff on the Matterhorn. We hit a bottleneck since the first move requires grabbing a heavy fixed rope and pulling yourself thirty feet up a precarious set of steel ladder rungs set into the rock face that leads to the top of the ledge. This can only be done one by one, so it pays to be first.

We climbed slowly for the next hour, traversing upward and across the massive East Face in the dark. A line of headlamps behind and ahead defined the trail, all slowly moving up the vertical face of the mountain. Shallow holds make the cliff face difficult, and following your guide's moves and hand and foot placements requires intense concentration. I was keenly aware of another climber immediately behind me for much of the way. I felt pressured to maintain my pace and concentration and it was challenging to do both simultaneously.

The rope teams continued as if choreographed, marching on, up and over ledges and around rock towers until dawn. Unlike my first climb in 1998, I was fatigued at this point. But the random side-to-side traverses on the East Face gave me brief respites from the relentless push upward. Helmut and I put on our crampons when we reached snow and ice. The scraping of metal on rock was unnerving, a jarring sound that disturbed the tranquil quiet. The sun began to rise across the Eastern panorama of the Pennine Alps, and we saw it peeking above the Mischabel peaks: Dom, Taschhorn, Alphubel, Rimpfischhorn and Strahlhorn. For me as a climber, the sun rising mid-climb always brings the optimistic feeling that I can make it to the summit.

Sunrise breaks over the Matterhorn: mid-climb right) and from the village of Zermatt (left): 2011

The Moseley Slabs are considered the two crux pitches on the Matterhorn, and just below the aerie perch of the Solvayhutte rescue shelter was the Lower Moseley Slab. Along with the Upper Moseley Slab, it is one of the hardest pitches on the mountain because it is steep, technical, awkward and exposed. At this point, Helmut and I moved off the East Face and rejoined the Hornli Ridge proper as the sun's rays reached the upper ramparts of the Matterhorn. Looking up, the summit block, the section of mountain that looks like a breaking wave, was glowing a brilliant golden color. I could see the entire way ahead and although I considered the difficulties we still had to face, it all seemed within reach. I was fatigued and not as agile as usual and working hard unlike in 1998. I was feeling the effects of the altitude and thin air acutely, but my inner drive kept me going

Helmut and I stopped for a drink of water on the narrow doorstep of the Solvayhutte. I was out of water, having used up my Camelback, the result of exertion without proper acclimatization. But I needed to hydrate. Helmut offered me a reviving drink and soon we were moving forward again up the second Moseley Slab crux and onto the shoulder. I have often described climbing the shoulder as ascending a steep church steeple that's covered with ice. You're at the edge looking down between your legs to thousands of feet of empty abyss, and as you climb you can feel the immense drop beneath your feet for its entire length. But instead of climbing a steeple that's a hundred feet above the ground, you're 3,000 feet above the Matterhorn Glacier. The memory of climbing this pitch scares me even today, perhaps because my two experiences on the shoulder were so vastly different. There are a series of iron rods along the shoulder used as belays. In 1998, Richard Andenmatten wrapped his rope around every belay point up the shoulder to guard my safety. This time Helmut and I advanced together on a moving belay, attached only to his rope and without the use of those protection points. I worried about what lay beyond that dangerous edge for our entire climb up the shoulder, mentally recalling my peril eleven years earlier on the North Face of the Breithorn.

Lower Moseley Slab (left) and Upper Moseley Slab (right); 2011

I'd forgotten how unforgiving the fixed rope sections of the summit block can be. There were about six pitches of steep rock chimneys that formed a three-sided enclosure. Heavy fixed ropes hung down the center. I searched for holds with one hand, while gripping the rope and hauling myself up with the other — all the while scraping the rock tower with the crampons on my boots. If the wind is blowing, it becomes especially precarious as it had been in 1998 when my crampon almost fell off my boot at this very spot.

By the time we reached the first fixed rope, I was exceedingly fatigued. My single-minded determination to summit was strong enough to override my exhaustion, and I tried not to become distracted from my goal. My father had died earlier that year and I had decided to bury some of his personal effects in the perpetual snow on top of the Matterhorn. That mission also drove me forward and I knew I still had to face seven long pitches ahead before we reached the upper roof and the summit snows.

FIXED ROPES ON THE MATTERHORN; 2011

Thankfully, there was little wind that day and we encountered no unexpected difficulties as we continued upward. I knew we were almost there when the statue of St. Bernard appeared, protruding from the snow like a welcome beacon on the North Face. We were on the upper roof, 4,000 feet above the Matterhorn Glacier, and a mere 50 yards from the summit. I felt the same elation I'd tasted thirteen years earlier as once again I stepped onto the knife-edge. Emotions overtook me: free falling tears followed the joy of a hard won victory.

I HONOR MY LATE FATHER AT THE MATTERHORN SUMMIT

I pulled off my pack and found my father's personal items. I remembered my dad as a tough disciplined Marine Corps veteran who was six foot two weighing in around 225 pounds. His nickname was "Big Beau" and this struck me as I dug a hole deep into the ridge. I placed and then covered his mementos with handfuls of snow. I said a prayer to my dad and then broke down crying, pouring out all my unresolved grief atop the Matterhorn. I explained the significance of the moment to Helmut. He was sympathetic and consoled me, but I can't recall his comforting words. As my grief subsided, I watched the next pairs of summiters crest the top of the peak and recognized the look of accomplishment on their faces.

This time we spent nearly an hour on top ("…one crowded hour of glorious life," to quote Whymper) taking in the perfect weather and the panorama of peaks and glaciers. Summiting for the second time was even sweeter than in 1998. I basked in my triumph. Helmut and I sat together eating our lunch on the edge of the Swiss summit, dangling our legs out in space as we gazed down thousands of feet to Italy at the base of the mountain. I was struck by the sharp contrast between Zermatt's charming wooden chalets and the concrete, bunker-style buildings that dotted the Italian village of Cervinia below. Yet no five-star meal anywhere in the world could compare to being on the summit of the Matterhorn and in such good company.

With Helmut on top of the Matterhorn - 2011

The peak became crowded so we began our descent, retracing our boot steps in the eternal snow. I no longer felt fatigued. Instead, a surge of energy came from my reserves. We encountered a bottleneck when we reached the fixed ropes. The line of climbers refused to relent. Helmut put me on belay and instructed me to rappel. I hesitated at first, not wanting to collide and injure someone with my crampon points, but I had little choice. As the climbers kept coming, I dropped into the chimney and did my best to avoid the onslaught. The first few pitches were similarly crowded, but after that the traffic subsided and we were once again on our own with the shoulder in sight ahead. In my moment of triumph and grief, I had forgotten about Ben and Jim. Now I wondered why I hadn't seen them among the crowd of summiters.

Looking down 4,000 feet at the fixed ropes and climbers

We came again to the Matterhorn's Shoulder. Descending its icy church steeple requires focus to be sure all ten points of each crampon bite securely into the hard surface at each step. My adrenaline surged as the edge drew near and its looming depth came into view. It was far scarier from this vantage point, as opposed to the ascent when you look up and forward. Helmut and I executed another rappel and worked our way down the pitch.

Once past the Lower Moseley Slab, the Matterhorn descent is a maze and finding the route is tricky. There are countless zigzags near the ridge and across the East Face that move left and right, over ledges and around rock towers. Climbers must spider down the steep sections with their backs facing the wall, using their arms and legs in a four point stance for stability. This is the Matterhorn's classic route which some guidebooks describe as "monotonous, especially in descent." The mountain continues to crumble piece by piece, day by day, from the constant freeze and thaw. It is important to be diligent and constantly on alert to avoid kicking loose stones down, and also to be ready to take cover when rocks fall from above. Helmut and I passed numerous faded slings and some rusty hardware dotting the correct route, left behind by others. There were false paths as well outside the traditional boundaries. Some of these past relics belonged to fallen climbers.

 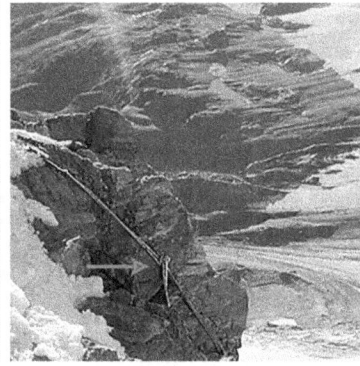

ROCK TOWERS ON THE MATTERHORN'S EAST FACE (LEFT).
OLD SLINGS AND HARDWARE LEFT BEHIND (RIGHT)

Our descent continued and soon we caught sight of the Hornlihutte several hundreds of feet below. The final zigzag parade across the East Face capped our extraordinary day. Stepping back onto the terrace of the Hornlihutte, I was proud to join the throngs taking in the mid-day sun on the terrace. I searched for Ben and Jim among the crowd, but I didn't see their faces. Helmut joined me inside and presented me with a golden Matterhorn climber badge and certificate of ascent that we both signed.² Kurt Lauber came up and told me of my friends' experiences on the mountain. Unfortunately, Ben had to turn back very early in the climb when he started vomiting severely — a victim of altitude sickness. Jim made it as far as the Solvayhutte, but a severe headache made continuing impossible. In the interest of safety, his guide Johann turned him around.

---

² Although I am not superstitious, I find it ironic that I now have a matched pair of certificates from two different years, and that the second climb was thirteen years after the first and on the thirteenth day of the month.

Inadequate acclimatization was the downfall for both Ben and Jim, a difficulty I could not have predicted or prevented. As I write this, Sam Branson, son of legendary billionaire adventurer Sir Richard Branson was recently airlifted from the summit of the Matterhorn by Air Zermatt due to altitude sickness.

Coming Full Circle

Having thanked Helmut, I gathered my pack and headed down the mountain toward Schwartzee once again feeling like a rock star. But it didn't take long before the toes on both my feet became inflamed, the result of repeatedly striking the front of my boots over the course of my rocky trek downward. With a few hours still to go before I'd reach the gondola station that would bring me back to Zermatt, I started to limp. As I hiked slowly downward, once again I heard the rotor blades of an Air Zermatt chopper rising from the valley below. It hovered around the Hornlihutte then rose up the East Face, circling the peak several times. I watched for several minutes, imagining another accident. I learned later that a climber in trouble was safely evacuated.

Despite my foot pain, the adrenaline surge from my summit spurred me forward, limping, toward the gondola. I climbed into an empty cabin and waited impatiently for it to start moving. A technical problem kept us grounded for at least fifteen minutes, so I looked back up toward the Matterhorn. I reveled in my climb much as I had in 1998, feeling immense satisfaction and that all was right with the world. This time, however, my thoughts quickly returned to Ben and Jim.

The gondola touched down at the far edge of Zermatt and I walked back to our apartment feeling both euphoria and compassion: jubilant, yet reserved. Once inside, Jim asked if I had summited and I was humbled by his simple question. I replied that I had, but I took pains to not over-elaborate on my triumph; a challenge, especially since I wanted to call Thea and share my success. Thea asked if Ben and Jim summited, and I told her quietly that they had not, not wanting them to overhear.

Don's guide had recommended waiting out the bad weather, and unfortunately like Jim and Ben, Don didn't summit either. That afternoon, he joined us at the apartment and I showed everyone my photographs of the climb. My camera had taken a lot of abuse on the fixed rope pitches, repeatedly banging on the rocks during my rappels. I had mixed feelings about showing the photos and talking about my success. After Don left, I didn't discuss my summit again. Don's disappointment fueled his return trip the following year when he successfully reached the top of the Matterhorn. I admired his persistence, passion, and also that climbing was an activity Don shared with his daughter. I could relate to his determination. It had taken me three attempts to summit the Matterhorn as well.

On his third attempt, my friend Don Coddington conquered the Matterhorn

At the start of the week, the three of us had been fired up to do numerous climbs. Our options seemed limitless, ranging from the traverse of the Breithorn, to Pollux and Castor or any number of lesser peaks. We were in an adventure mecca. But after the trials of the Matterhorn, all three of us were ready to leave. We embraced a change of plans and researched tropical alternatives, ultimately deciding to finish our trip in Ibiza, Spain by way of Milan.

I couldn't help but appreciate that the unplanned side trip to Milan brought my Matterhorn adventures full circle. I had been a student living in Milan in 1988 when I first saw the mountain that inspired an adventure that would span more than 25 years. I was eager to walk the streets of Milan again and to introduce Ben and Jim to my former haunts. We rolled into Stazione Centrale, one of Europe's largest and most bustling train stations made entirely of Italian marble. Leaving the station, we walked a route I had taken numerous times years ago. I used to walk the city randomly all day not caring where I would end up.

I stopped outside my favorite trattoria, *A Sante Lucia*, but was disappointed to find it barricaded behind a metal grate. I approached a street vendor and politely inquired in my rusty Italian,

"Per favore, A Sante Lucia – Chiuso? (Is it closed?)"

"Chiuso," was his reply and he quickly turned his attention to a paying customer.

We moved on, settling for a leisurely lunch at a sidewalk café just up the promenade from the Duomo, Milan's centuries-old cathedral. All facets of Italian life from impeccably attired businessmen to teenagers in love passed by us as we dined on pasta and San Pellegrino, and I relived memories from decades past. Suddenly I was 26 again with a world of unlimited possibilities ahead.

I thought about the paths that had led our group to the Alps and about what each of us took away from the trip. For Jim, just making the attempt had been a worthwhile experience. Ben had added a new and dramatic story to his repertoire. I felt grateful to have successfully overcome my accident, and summiting was all the more meaningful by honoring my father on top of the Matterhorn.

EPILOGUE

It has been said that fear keeps you alive when you are pushing your limits. When I was on the North Face of the Breithorn and my crampons and axes were insecurely attached to the ice, I had no doubt I was at the absolute limit of my fear and my capability. Seconds felt like minutes as I anxiously watched my guide Helmut thread in an ice screw to secure us before we both peeled off the mountain. It is surreal to reach those limits and come back safely to tell the story. When I think of the Matterhorn today, it still scares me. Am I capable of climbing it? Yes. Is its danger diminished by my firsthand knowledge? Of course not.

I question why I keep climbing. Every time I do, in the rush I find myself imagining the worst and I rediscover my own fears. I look at the rope, my lifeline, and think it might sever on the jagged rock above; I question if my harness is secured properly, even though I check it before ascending. Will my equipment fail on a rappel and send me into another free fall - to certain injury or my possible death? These thoughts must be aftermath of my accident. The specter of danger feels stronger now than it did even during my first climbs immediately following my 2009 fall. It seems logical, for me at least, that fear and caution magnify with age.

Why am I still drawn to climbing? Why does my inner voice continue to call me to the mountains? The answer, of course, is passion. Climbing is so many things to me: the look and feel of the equipment and pride in its proper use. It offers a chance to lose myself and my problems in the delicate movements of the challenge. There is the feeling of reaching the edge and looking past, or being motionless on the wall and surveying the depths below… they all feed my soul.

As I age I am naturally slowing down, and although I'm 52 as I'm writing this, I feel 15. I am still a strong, fluid skier, but I am no longer able to perform the aerial tricks I once mastered. Instead, simply cruising down steep mountainsides with graceful, arcing turns fulfills me now. I was once a competent open water scuba diver, but over the last few years I have developed a paranoia that must be overcome before I am comfortable on deeper dives. I know also that I can no longer climb at an advanced level. My moves are not as graceful, and there are certain climbs I once made that I am not sure I could repeat today. This is alright for now, as long as I can still find fulfillment in my passion, but how will I feel when I am older and have nothing but my memories? I have difficulty accepting the normal progression of life and the reality that I'm slowing down. Despite that my need to climb once led to a serious injury, the thought of leading an ordinary life as I age, without adventure, feels inadequate.

For a long time a spectacular peak called the Weisshorn has been on my bucket list. Its icy white shroud is visible from the Glacier Express, guarding the approach to Zermatt. While the Matterhorn is 4-sided, the Weisshorn is a 3-sided pyramid of faces and ridges. Its notoriety comes from being the second to last alpine peak to have been ascended during the Golden Age of Mountaineering. The approach to its own Weisshornhutte is much longer than on other Alpine peaks, and there is ever-present exposure on its long summit route.

Could I possibly train hard enough to make it? Would my foot act up again and cause troubles on the long descent? Is it even prudent to consider the climb at this stage in my life and as a father with a young family? My doubts return and my inner conflict persists.

My daughters Samantha and Madison delight me with their curiosity, fearlessness and appetite for adventure. Years ago when they were toddlers, I beamed when they climbed our stone fireplace or the boulder wall which borders our driveway. I would get down to their eye level, survey the route and marvel at their moves and natural ability. As they've grown, their skills have developed. Ten-year-old Sam goes to the indoor rock gym after school, and I am amazed at her core strength and natural skill as she ascends overhangs. Madison, now eight, likes to scale the peak of our house. What are their limits? Will we climb anything significant together? Is the Matterhorn in our future? Time will tell.

I will encourage my daughters to climb and pursue their own adventurous dreams, wherever they lead. I hope I am an inspiration to them. Over the years, I have maintained my fitness and believe that I can still climb routes of moderate difficulty. This has been one of the benefits of my years of travel and adventure. Climbing has meant the world to me. If you also wonder, *"Can I do this?,"* I wholeheartedly believe that you can. Follow your path, get proper instruction, prepare well and hire a reputable guide.

Everyone has a Matterhorn in life, mountain or not, and yours is out there waiting. You can achieve seemingly impossible dreams, if you believe and strive forward. The journey will be worth the effort.

Climbing in and around our home with
daughters Samantha (left) and Madison (right)

"Climb if you will, but remember that courage and strength are nought without prudence, and that a momentary negligence may destroy the happiness of a lifetime. Do nothing in haste; look well to each step; and from the beginning think what may be the end".

Reprinted from *Scrambles Amongst the Alps in the Years 1860 – 1869* by Edward Whymper 2010 Nabu Press

RESOURCES

An Inside View Of Zermatt

Zermatt is fascinating. Amidst the constant new construction, mostly contemporary glass, wooden and steel structures, the village has grown around historic century-old chalets preserved for posterity. Luxury and poverty co-exist in dramatic contrast, side by side. Generations continue their ancestor's work in meadows within sight of 5-Star hotels and shops that cater to the ultra-wealthy. Every class in between can also find something in Zermatt. Millions of tourists from around the globe take in the magnificent view of the peaks from the ease and convenience of the Gornergrat train and numerous other trams and gondolas. Alpine climbers and trekkers are quick to leave the village behind to head out to the serenity of the high alpine huts (buttes) and refuges.

In the summer, all the national alpine ski teams arrive for weeks to hone their skills and speed on the Theodul Glacier in preparation for the coming World-Cup season. Anyone can rent equipment and ski side-by-side Olympic champions or others who soon will be.

Zermatt thrives, continues to grow, and appears recession proof because the Matterhorn itself is the magnetic draw. Tourist numbers keep climbing and as a result, more and more accommodations and amenities arrive each season.

Enchanted village beneath the magic mountain

Tourists from around the world are drawn to Zermatt for the grandeur of the Matterhorn and the area's spectacular scenery. A rack railway trip up the mountain to the Gornergrat Hotel offers sweeping views of glaciers and a panorama of 4,000 meter peaks. The Gornergrat is a hotel and observatory situated on a rocky pinnacle that overlooks five distinct 4,000 thousanders: Monte Rosa, Lyskamm, Castor, Pollux and the Breithorn. The Monte Rosa Glacier and its satellite glaciers spill down before the Gornergrat in a wide swath of eternal ice. Hordes of tourists pour out of the trains and jockey for position to get the best photos. Avalanches frequently thunder down the steep couloirs and over the rocks, visible from the Gornergrat Hotel's busy outdoor café. It's a spectacular vantage point to take in the peaks and glaciers and for people watching visitors from all nations.

Zermatt is a walking village. To protect the pure mountain air from being spoiled by the outside world, cars are banned in favor of electric carts that transport people and supplies. The carts are barely audible until they're almost on top of you. Only the local physician can keep a car in the village. The public must leave their cars in a massive car park in the nearby village of Tasch.

In the village, the Alpine Museum captures the history of Zermatt and of climbing in the region. A highlight is memorabilia from the first ascent of the Matterhorn in 1865 and the story of the tragic disaster on the descent. The collection includes the broken rope from the fall, one of the climber's hob nailed boots and the hat belonging to lead Chamonix guide Michel Croz. Miscellaneous boots, flasks, axes and gear found on the mountain from numerous climbs are also on display. The first climbers to reach the summits of the local peaks were British, and the English helped spark the tourist boom to Zermatt. They have long considered Zermatt a second home and even have their own church presided over by a proper Vicar.

Fascinating places are found in every street and alleyway. The hotels and wooden chalets are adorned with flowers of every hue. Wealthy hotel families live in close proximity to the hard working farm families who live as their earlier ancestors did without electric lights or modern conveniences. You can hear cowbells from high up on the alpine meadows and yes, the chocolate tastes better in Zermatt.

ZERMATT-AREA TRAINING HIKES & CLIMBS

The following information will help you prepare should you wish to climb the Matterhorn or another peak. Before undertaking a climb of this magnitude, you'll need to spend months hiking steep trails and getting into strong cardiovascular shape. Excursions in Zermatt challenge even the fittest hiker, and the Alpine Center of Zermatt recommends spending several days to acclimate to the altitude before your first climb. Basic preparation should include hiking a minimum of a thousand to two thousand vertical feet per hour with occasional rest stops. The Zermatt trail network has signposts along the way to mark the standard time to reach a particular destination. If you are highly motivated and move particularly fast, it is possible to cut these standard times in half. If you can manage this accelerated pace on a few of the more challenging hikes, then you are fit to climb a 4,000 meter peak.

Although I have frequently trained alone on these expeditions, hiking with a companion is recommended. Many hikes on these high alpine peaks take you to remote areas with few visitors. On solo hikes, a simple slip or turned ankle could put you in an extremely serious predicament. It is always prudent to inform someone of your intended destination and your approximate time of return. I suggest purchasing Rescue Insurance from Air Zermatt at a reasonable fee. Without this insurance, airlift by helicopter will be prohibitively expensive.

Several of the excursions detailed below will bring you to altitudes of between 3,000 and 3,400 meters and offer excellent preparation for the Matterhorn or another of the 4,000 meter peaks in the Zermatt area. A good map of all high alpine trails is available at the Alpine Center for one Swiss Franc.

> **Gornergrat Hike**
> Difficulty: medium to strenuous
> Standard time: 4-5 hours one-way

From Bahnhofstrasse, follow the river south to the end of the village. Cross the bridge to Winkelmatten, following signposts up through pine forests to Moos, Ritti, then on to Riffelalp at 2,222 meters. High up on the cliff top you will see the Riffelberg hotel, your next destination and a good spot for a snack. Hopefully, you've brought some energy bars or trail mix, as food and drink at the Riffelberg is priced for the view. Climbing up past Riffelberg, follow the track of the Gornergrat Railway, past Rotenboden Station and the Riffelhorn (a small rock peak used by the Zermatt Guides for Matterhorn training) until you reach Gornergrat. The Gornergrat features the most famous glacial panorama in Europe. From this lofty vantage point, travelers marvel at the massive glaciers which converge hundreds of feet below.

> **Mettelhorn Hike**
> Difficulty: strenuous (crampons and trekking poles strongly recommended)
> Standard time: 4-5 hours, one-way

Next to Grampy's Bar on Bahnhofstrasse in Zermatt is a paved walkway that leads to a dirt path trail up the Trift Valley. Your ultimate goal is a small but steep mountain at the edge of a short glacier with an amazing panoramic view of all the four thousand meter peaks, dominated by the Matterhorn's imposing North Face.

This hike zigzags steeply up to the Edelweiss Restaurant, which sits on a cliff top five hundred feet above the village. At night, the red and white lights of the Edelweiss can be seen from quite a distance. Continuing past the Edelweiss, the trail follows the Triftbach, a cascading river of glacial melt that plummets down the steep mountainside on its way through the center of Zermatt, down the Visp valley and ultimately into the Rhone, one of Europe's larger rivers.

Upon reaching the plateau, the small yet comfortable Trift Hotel offers a hearty meal and a friendly greeting from the owner and his family. *Hotel* is a misnomer as the lodging provided is simple with few conveniences. The building is weather-beaten but offers refuge from the summer storms that often blow through the area.

The Trift Hotel

At the Trift, the path forks in two. The left side leads towards the Hohbalmen and an extremely exposed expedition, best saved for another day. Instead, continue to the right where the trail winds steeply up towards the Mettelhorn. You will pass through another small valley surrounded by a number of lesser peaks on both sides as you climb. This area is especially remote and is not a good place to be during lightning storms. Eventually you will reach a small glacier that is crevasse-free. Unless there has been a recent snowfall, there will be a trodden path across the glacier leading to a steep zigzag path up the Mettelhorn. Within approximately 20 minutes, you will be on top of the pointy little peak. If the weather is clear, the panorama of peaks includes the village of Zermatt far below.

The Mettelhorn has not been immune to the adverse effects of global warming, and in recent years the snow trail has been reduced to a thin layer of ice covering jagged rocks. To prevent dangerous slips, crampons and trekking poles are a must for a safe hike across this glacier.

> **Oberrothorn Hike**
> Difficulty: strenuous
> Standard time: 4 - 5 hours, one-way

From the old section of Zermatt, cross the river and head north a few blocks. At the bakery, turn right and follow the paved walkway uphill until the path turns to dirt. Continue through larch pine forests to the hamlet of Ried. Follow signs to Tuftern at 2,209 meters. Heading north, follow the path leading to both Unterrothorn and Oberrothorn. You will eventually reach a fork that splits toward each of these peaks. The right fork takes you up and over the Unterrothorn, which is the upper terminus of the Rothorn Cable Car. Hiking down the backside leads to a steep path up to the summit of the Oberrothorn. Along the steep trail just below the summit, there is a series of metal and glass kinetic sculptures that depict the mineral, plant, animal, human, and spiritual worlds with text in four languages. From the summit itself, there is a spectacular view of the icy veil of the Weisshorn, twin summits of the Rimpfischhorn, Monte Rosa (the highest peak in Switzerland), the Breithorn Massif and the Matterhorn. Choosing the left fork bypasses the Unterrothorn, and leads to the base of Oberrothorn.

> **Hohbalmen/Schonbuhlhutte Hike**
> Difficulty: very strenuous
> Standard time: 6 hours, one-way

Begin this hike heading up to the Trift Hotel. At the Trift, bear left and climb steadily up the path to reach the high mountain terrace that leads towards the spectacular North Face of the Matterhorn. Move at a steady pace and do not linger, especially if the weather seems turbulent, as there can be lightning danger. The path descends to Kalbermatten at the lower edge of the Zmutt Glacier and continues upward to the Schonbuhlhutte, a climber's refuge at the base of the Matterhorn North Face and peak of Dent D'Herens. Return to Zermatt through the hamlet of Zmutt. If weather is threatening or time is short, an hour can be shaved off in both directions by proceeding back down the Zmutt valley to Zermatt at Kalbermatten.

> **Riffelhorn Climb (technical)**
> Difficulty: varies depending on route
> Standard time: varies, ranging from 15-60 minutes

The Riffelhorn is a small rock peak located high above Zermatt, used by the local guides to assess a climber's rock climbing ability before leading him or her on any serious mountain. There are numerous climbs for all abilities with several routes that duplicate difficulties on the Matterhorn. The Riffelhorn is excellent training for the Matterhorn climb itself. Inquire: Alpine Center Zermatt, Bahnhofstrasse.

> **Breithorn Climb (non-technical)**
> Difficulty: semi-strenuous
> Standard time: 2 hours, one-way
> from the Kleine Matterhorn starting point

The Breithorn has been dubbed the "easiest 4,000 meter peak in the Alps," but don't take this lightly. There are numerous crevasses on the approach and without a guide, it is easy to become disoriented on the flanks of the mountain in bad weather or fog. Climbing the Breithorn is a good test of stamina and is helpful when acclimating for more serious climbs. It has been described as a snow plod, but it can be icy at times. It is a strenuous, fairly steep hike requiring crampons at altitude. Exposure is nonexistent on the ascent, but once on the summit, one can look thousands of feet down the treacherous North Face if close to the edge. The Breithorn is popular. On a clear day several hundred people will climb to its summit from the line of first ascent – the classic route. Inquire: Alpine Center Zermatt, Bahnhofstrasse

Breithorn Classic Route

Pollux Climb (technical)
Difficulty: challenging
Standard time: 4 hours, one-way
from the Kleine Matterhorn

Pollux is a mixed climb of snow, rock and ice that is a challenging expedition for the first time mountaineer. The Zermatt Guides lead this climb each week with a maximum of two climbers per rope. The climb begins from the Kleine Matterhorn Cable Car station and follows the glacier along the Swiss/Italian frontier for about 90 minutes until reaching the peak. There are fixed ropes and chain at some of the trickier rock sections. The crux of the climb to the summit involves traversing a delicate knife-edge ridge that falls away for thousands of feet on either side. The slightest gust of wind makes this a very exciting passage. Descent is from a snow/ice field on the opposite side of the mountain from the side ascended. Inquire: Alpine Center Zermatt, Bahnhofstrasse.

> **Rimpfischhorn Climb**
> **(Long, strenuous approach/technical)**
> Difficulty: advanced. Standard time: 6-7 hours from the Fluealp to the summit, one-way.

The Rimpfischhorn is perhaps the best training climb to prepare for the Matterhorn. Its long approach is a test of stamina. The steep rock, ice and exposure challenge all but the most experienced mountaineers. The Rimpfischhorn has two prominent summits. Ascending the highest point involves tackling a steep ice climb and technical rocks and then continuing up and over the lower summit to a saddle until you reach the higher summit. Inquire: Alpine Center Zermatt, Bahnhofstrasse.

HOW TO CLIMB:
COMMON METHODS, SKILLS AND TIPS

TOP ROPE CLIMBING

Top roping consists of hiking to the top of the rock face from an easy approach and setting up an anchor system attached to large trees or rocks with carabiners (D-shaped metal rings which hold the rope) and a series of slings made of nylon webbing. In a top rope setup, the rope passes up the crag and through two carabiners held by the slings at the top, then back down to the ground. The climber ties the rope to his waist harness, while the belayer who stays on the ground passes the other end of the rope through his belay device. As the climber ascends, the belayer takes in the slack in the rope, keeping a taught line on the climber. If the climber slips from his holds, the belayer can stop the slip instantaneously and limit the length of the fall. When the climber reaches the top of the crag, he simply leans back in his harness and walks slowly down the wall (rapelling) while the belayer lowers him safely to the ground safely. Both climber and belayer communicate with a series of commands such as *on belay, belay on, climbing, slack, and rapping.* Top roping provides all the thrills of climbing with safety and simplicity, but is limited to about 80 to 90 feet or half the length of a typical climbing rope.

LEAD CLIMBING

Lead climbing is far more committing and requires significantly more training and skill. When lead climbing, there is no limit to the height climbers can ascend as they climb pitch by pitch. The leader ascends, belayed from below by a partner who takes in the rope. Every ten feet or so, the leader places "pro" (protection devices such as wire nuts, camming/expansion units) in cracks or features of the rock as he or she rises. Once a piece of protection has been placed, the leader clips his rope into the piece and climbs up to the next spot to place protection. When the leader reaches the end of each pitch, he ties in to secure himself to the rock, then signals for his partner (the second climber on the rope) to begin climbing. The second climber removes and collects each piece of protection as he meets it, while being belayed from above by the first climber. The lead climber belays the second by taking in the rope while the second climber ascends. When the second reaches the leader's stance, he also ties in before the next pitch is attempted in the same way.

It is far safer to be the second on the rope, as the second climber is belayed and protected completely by the leader above. If the leader falls when climbing a pitch, the length of his fall depends upon how high he is above the last piece of protection placed. He will fall twice that distance; falling the length above the protection, and then the same distance again past it until the rope is arrested by that piece of protection. Placing protection is an exacting task. There is no guarantee that the placement is fail-safe. Only one piece of protection is placed at each point with no backup. To descend, ropes are attached to anchors which the climber then rappels down. When both climbers reach the bottom of the pitch, the rope is pulled down through the anchor, coiled and re-secured to rappel the next pitches in the same fashion all the way to the bottom of the climb.

ALPINE STYLE MOUNTAINEERING

In Mountaineering there are also two styles of climbing. Alpine style is similar to lead climbing, as both climbers ascend pitches and protect each other as they climb. When the pitch is not deemed particularly dangerous, time is saved by climbing together simultaneously in a "moving belay." If the climb is long, or bad weather sets in, a bivouac is undertaken. Bivouacing involves finding a secure sheltered place on the mountain to pass several hours or spend the night. If a suitable place is not found, the climbers will attach themselves to the wall with hardware and protection, covering themselves with wind and waterproof garments or equipment known as a bivi bag. Climbers descend the mountain either on a moving or protected belay in similar fashion

EXPEDITION STYLE MOUNTAINEERING

Expedition style climbing involves a long climb at significant altitude with stays along the route at a series of higher camps, supplied as the climbers ascend. During the acclimatization process, climbers get used to the thinning air as they rise from basecamp to higher and higher camps. A summit bid is finally attempted from the highest camp when climbers are fully acclimatized and snow conditions and weather are stable. The camps serve as a shelter when the weather remains bad for extended periods of time.

GEAR AND SUPPLIES

Most of the gear you will need can be found at a good outdoor adventure store or mountaineering shop. Eastern Mountain Sports (EMS) has many locations in the northeast, and Recreational Equipment Inc. (REI) has locations nationwide. Both are staffed by knowledgeable, outdoors people and have everything you need for any outdoor pursuit. The vast selection includes top-brands and each store's own line of private label gear and clothing at reasonable prices.

Boots: First and foremost, one needs a good fitting pair of rugged boots with strong support and traction. Boots come in varieties designed for different uses. Backpacking or trail boots provide comfort and support, but they lack the rigidity needed for technical routes, and they do not have the correct sole pattern and lugs in both the front and rear to attach and properly fit crampons. If this is the case, opt for a decent mountaineering boot which is more expensive but also more versatile. You can both hike and climb in a mountaineering boot.

Wear new boots around the house and yard before hiking on serious terrain to break them in. Wool/nylon blend socks without holes or darnings wick moisture away from the skin and are a boot's best friend. Blisters are the enemy on a trail and especially high up a mountainside. Crampons are necessary on most mountain climbs and can be rented at any sport shop in Zermatt.

Shell or Anorak. Next, a wind and rainproof shell or anorak and lightweight pants protect you from all but a deluge. Not only will they help you keep dry, but they insulate you from the chilling effects of wind. A fleece pullover, shirt or zip up will serve as your warmth layer. Long underwear or polypropylene (polypro) tops and bottoms are designed to wick moisture away from the skin, then evaporate before you get chilled. T-shirts are not recommended for any but the shortest walks as they tend to stay wet when you sweat. The old expression "cotton kills" means exactly that; falling temperatures and wet clothing lead to hypothermia.

Hat and gloves. A warm winter hat and lightweight gloves take up little space in a pack, prevent heat loss from extremities and provide great comfort and protection in an unexpected storm. A rescue blanket is the size of a baseball card when folded, but opens up to a shiny silver poncho that insulates you from the wind and is visible to rescuers from a long distance.

Packs come in all sizes and shapes for many uses. Day packs have limited features and generally offer little more than a pocket or two and shoulder straps. A good mountaineering pack will have a medium to large capacity, several smaller zip pockets, a good support system such as hip and chest belts and a variety of carry loops for skis, walking sticks, ice axes and other tools. Talk to an expert about your intended use before selecting a pack. Once you find the one you like, put some weight in it and carry it around the store. Imagine yourself on an all-day trek in the high country. Will it be comfortable on your back for many hours? Is its profile low enough to help you keep your balance? Is it likely to get caught on a rock during a climb?

Utility knives take up little room but can be a life-saver. Multi-bladed tools may include cutting blades, pliers, scissors, screwdrivers, can openers, saws, corkscrews and more. Some of the best are the typical Swiss Army knives by Victorinox or Wenger, or American-made Leatherman tools. Always carry a utility tool in your pack.

Ice axe. Carry a high quality metal or wooden ice axe on all steep snow and ice climbs to aid in self-arrest if you slip. The bottom of the shaft will have a spiked point to penetrate snow, while the double sided head consists of a serrated blade and an adze or shovel tip. If a climber falls on a steep slope, he immediately plunges the serrated blade into the snow or ice and puts all weight on the blade to maximize friction and arrest the fall. The adze is used to cut steps in steep snow or ice walls for added security on a climb, or to rid rocky handholds of an ice coating.

Trekking poles have become popular over the past few years. They have a telescopic feature that allows length adjustment for comfort and helps them stow easily on a pack. Poles give you added security over rocky, technical hiking terrain and provide a strong core workout. Trekking poles are essential if a hiker develops a knee or ankle injury, and especially if you get hurt in a remote area.

Food and water are essential. For a long day hike, carry at least two liters of water in trail bottles that can be attached to or carried in your pack. A hydration system such as Camelbak fits compactly inside your pack and is lighter than multiple bottles. Hydrate often and always have a plan for where to refill your water supply. If you are not sure of the next refill source, save water to get yourself back down the hill. Sterilization tablets let you drink safely from any stream. It's essential to pack light, so forget the Jiffy Pop in favor of energy bars, trail mix in zip-lock bags or peanut butter sandwiches. Carry enough food to last a day or two in case you get lost or injured and need to bivi overnight where you are.

First aid kit. Carry a basic first aid kit with bandages, anti-bacterial disinfectant, tape and an ace bandage to provide compression and support should you twist or sprain an ankle. Carry a good local map of the terrain and a professional whistle on all your hikes so you can signal for help if disabled or lost.

Speaking from personal experience, I am always amazed at the horde of summer hikers who show up at Pinkham Notch Base Camp on the lower slopes of Mt. Washington in New Hampshire, a summit that boasts some of the most severe weather in the world. Many lack adequate gear, food and water. You can see them hiking above tree line in nothing but T-shirts, shorts and Teva sandals. Perfect summer weather on the lower slopes can be misleading since above the tree line summer storms can come quickly, and the temperatures can plummet as the wind rises. Over the years more than a few hikers have perished on Mt. Washington when ill-preparedness led to hypothermia.

MATTERHORN TRAINING

Physical fitness is of the utmost importance in mountaineering. It's important for safety, but also to get the most enjoyment from a climb. Climbing is exerting and in most cases, you will hike uphill for hours before you reach the mountain you want to climb.

To get in shape for climbing, cross-training is generally best. I swim the breaststroke, lift weights, trail run, mountain bike and hike for months preceding a major climb. I find it motivating to pretend I am on the actual climb when I train. As the climb gets nearer, my training intensifies with my level of fitness.

Most people hate to work out because it is difficult and it takes effort to see results. I have always felt better about myself the more fit I am. You look better and feel better and are healthier. You have more energy and can do more. It doesn't take long to lose your fitness when you become inactive. Becoming fit is like any other goal in life: it's a mindset. When you set your mind to something, you can achieve it.

To train for the Matterhorn, I started with a simple calendar/day planner. In the months preceding my trip to Zermatt, I chronicled each day's workout and listed the activity, the mileage, the duration, any unique obstacles encountered, and how I felt during and after the activity. I repeated my favorite activities several times and enjoyed looking back on the calendar daily to follow my fitness and watch my times improve as my preparation progressed.

Training is unique to each person. Some people like to bike, run, or hike. Others prefer indoor gyms, stair climbers and treadmills. I offer my own five month Matterhorn schedule below as an example of a tried and true regimen.

Month One
- 14 Mile Road Bike Ride – 50 minutes (two days)
- Mogul Skiing – 2 hours (ten days)
- 3 Mile Run – 32 minutes (one day)

Month Two
- Climbed steep woods next to Black Diamond ski trail – 2,000 vertical feet - straightest line possible – 90 minutes (one day)

- Climbed Black Diamond ski trail up the snow – 2,000 vertical feet – 90 minutes (one day)
- Mogul Skiing – 2 hours (five days)
- 14 Mile Road Bike Ride – 50 minutes (one day)
- Mountain Trail Run – 1,200 vertical feet (one day)
- Mountain Trail Run – 3.5 miles - 55 minutes (one day)
- Mountain Bike Ride variable terrain – 4 miles – 45 minutes (five days)
- Mountain Bike ride around Boston – 14 miles – three hours (one day)
- Jogged up Black Diamond ski trail on snow/glissade down – 2,000 vertical feet – 55 minutes (three days)

Month Three
- Mountain Bike on logging roads, variable terrain – 4 miles – 45 minutes (ten days)
- Weight Lifting – 115 pounds bench press – 300 reps (fifteen days)
- Jogged up/down Black Diamond ski trail – 2,000 vertical feet – 55 minutes (four days)
- Road Bike 32 miles with steep climb – 90 minutes (two days)
- Trail Run variable terrain – 3 miles – 35 minutes (four days)
- Hiked steep trail – 4.5 miles – 80 minutes (one day)

Month Four
- Weight Lifting – 115 pounds bench press – 360 reps (twelve days)
- Beach run three miles – 30 minutes (one day)
- 38 mile Road Bike Ride – 100 minutes (two days)
- Mountain Bike Ride in Boston – 22 miles – 3.5 hours (one day)
- Mountain Bike Ride variable terrain – 5 miles – one hour (eight days)
- Hiked on ski trails variable terrain – 2 hours (two days)
- Jogged up Black Diamond ski trail – 2,000 vertical feet – 50 minutes (three days)
- Chairlift Tower climbing for heights and dexterity – half hour

(one day)
- Speed Hike to summit of Mt Washington, NH – 2 hours, 9 minutes. Down hike 90 minutes (one day)
- Tennis Match – 2 hours (one day)

Month Five
- Weight Lifting – 115 pounds bench press – 360 reps (three days)
- Trail Run on ski trails – 3 miles – 45 minutes (two days)
- Mountain Bike variable terrain – 3 miles – thirty minutes (3 days)
- Hiked in Zermatt Winklematten/Furi/Zmutt – 8 miles at leisurely pace (one day)
- Hiked in Zermatt (Oberrothorn) – 12 miles – six hours (one day)
- Hiked in Zermatt (Rotenboden) to base of Riffelhorn - rock climb several routes on Riffelhorn with guide Richard Andenmatten (one day)
- Swimming and Jacuzzi in Hotel Eden Pool (three hours)

Climb the Matterhorn – 3 hours 20 minutes to summit, 3 hours descent

DICTIONARY OF CLIMBING TERMS

Avalanche – Unstable snow layer upon older firm layer on a steep slope is released and slides downhill gaining momentum and power while burying everything in its path

Belay – Protecting a climber from a potential fall using ropes, friction devices and/or other hardware

Belay Device – A metal device used to protect the climber which creates friction on the rope and is in the complete control of the belayer. The device also allows safe and controlled rappelling down a cliff face.

Bergshrund – A crevasse creating a gap against the face of a mountain caused by the glacier moving downhill parallel to the mountain.

Carabiner – A "D" shaped spring loaded metal device used to attach a belay device to a climbing harness, a sling to a piece of protection to attach to the rock or to secure the rope in a top–rope situation.

Chimney – A rock feature of 2 or 3 sides which can be ascended by placing hands and feet against the walls using opposing pressure.

Cirque – A bowl–shaped concave feature of a mountainside carved out by glaciers during the ice age.

Cornice– Windblown snow that accumulates deeply over the edge of a steep cliff face and hangs precariously until it eventually lets go and plunges down the mountainside.

Crampon – A metal platform with 10 or 12 sharp spikes protruding downward that attaches to the bottom of mountaineering boots allowing one to walk or climb on steep ice.

Crevasse – A deep gap in the surface of ice caused by the constant downward movement of the glacier

Crux or Crux Pitch – The most technically challenging pitch or feature of a climb.

Glacier – Layers upon layers of perpetual snow and ice in very slow but constant downward movement.

Ice Screw – A threaded metal protection device which can be screwed deep into the ice with an eye to attach a carabiner and rope used to belay or protect a climbing party.

Ice Tool – Short handled axe used to facilitate upward movement on a steep ice face by swinging the pick end into the ice.

Ice Axe – Long handled axe used for walking support on glaciers and to arrest a fall.

Moraine – Rocky debris released from and deposited on the sides of glaciers as the glacier travels downhill.

Peeled or Peel Off – To slip from one's holds and fall.

Posthole – Stepping into loose and deep snow (verb) or a hole in deep snow caused from footsteps (noun)

Protection – Mechanical devices used to protect a climber from a fall or used in a rappel.

Saddle – Depression between two mountain peaks.

Scrambling – Ascending fairly steep rock features that do not generally require ropes or other protection.

Scree – Loose unstable rock of differing sizes deposited on a steep hillside from crumbling cliff faces above.

Sling – Static nylon webbing either pre-fabricated in a loop of determined length or in a flat length that can be tied end to end used with carabiners and other pieces of protection to safeguard and limit the fall of a climber.

Technical – Challenging or hazardous terrain that requires the use of ropes and other protection.

Verglas – Thin layer or coating of ice over rock caused by freezing rain or melt.

GUIDES AND INSTRUCTION

Alpine Center Zermatt, P.O. Box 403
CH-3920 Zermatt, Switzerland
Ph: +41 (0) 27 966 24 60   Fax: +41 (0) 27 966 24 69
Email: alpincenter@zermatt.ch
Home page: www.alpincenter-zermatt.ch/en/welcome/
Guide page: www.alpincenter-zermatt.ch/active_mountain_guides.html

Exum Mountain Guides, Grand Teton National Park, P.O. Box 56
Moose, Wyoming 83012
Ph: 307-733-2297 Fax 307-733-9613
Email: exum@wyoming.com
www.exumguides.com

Eastern Mountain Sports (EMS)
Climbing School North Conway, NH and New Paltz, NY
Ph: 800-310-4504   www.emsclimb.com
Retail Stores www.ems.com

Books
The Alpine 4000 Meter Peaks by the Classic Routes, Richard Goedeke, Diadem Books - London, Menasha Ridge Press – Alabama, 1991

Scrambles Amongst the Alps, Edward Whymper, Ten Speed Press – California, 1981

Men and the Matterhorn, Gaston Rebuffat, Oxford University Press – New York, 1973

The Eiger Obsession, John Harlin III, Simon & Schuster – New York, 2007

Straight Up, James Ramsey Ulman, Doubleday – New York, 1968 (Out of Print) Try Alibris.com, Chesslerbooks.com or a local library.

The Climb Up To Hell, Jack Olsen, St. Martin's Paperbacks, 2000

Never a Bad Word or a Twisted Rope, Glenn Exum, Grand Teton Natural History Association – Wyoming, 1998

Teewinot, A Year In The Teton Range, Jack Turner, St. Martin's Press, NY, 2000

Banner In the Sky, James Ramsey Ulman, Harper Keypoint - New York, 1988

The Beckoning Silence, Joe Simpson, The Mountaineers Books – Seattle, 2003

Zermatt Saga, Cicely Williams, Rotten Verlag – Brig Switzerland, 1989

The White Spider, Heinrich Harrer, Paladin/Harper Collins – London, 1983

Ulrich Inderbinen, As Old As the Century," Heidi Lanz and Liliane DeMeester, Southgate Publishers, 1997

Films
The Alps, Macgillivray Freeman Films, 2007 www.alpsfilm.com

Third Man On The Mountain, Walt Disney Co., Buena Vista Home Entertainment www.disneydvd.com

K2, The Ultimate High, Paramount Pictures, 1992

North Face, Music Box Films, 2010

The Beckoning Silence, Life and Death On the Eiger, British Television Film, 2007

The Eiger Sanction, Universal Pictures, 1975

ABOUT THE AUTHOR

Roger Beaudoin, entrepreneur and adventurer, was born in Holyoke, Massachusetts and discovered the woods at an early age. In graduate school at Babson College in Massachusetts he became interested in hiking and while living in Italy for the summer, discovered the iconic Matterhorn in Zermatt, Switzerland. This fueled his ambition to climb the famous peak and his lifelong obsession with the mountain.

Roger continues to rock and ice climb today and may return to Zermatt one day to once again ascend the Matterhorn hopefully with his daughters. There are, as well, a few other peaks that remain on his bucket list.

www.ingramcontent.com/pod-product-compliance
Lightning Source LLC
Chambersburg PA
CBHW062226080426
42734CB00010B/2047